COVERED IN CATS

COVERED IN CATS

Stories of Felines and Other Astounding Beings

Anita Camera

Covered in Cats: Stories of Felines and Other Astounding Beings
Copyright © 2020 by Anita Camera

All images by author except those used by kind permission.

ISBN 978-1-952194-06-1

Design by River Sanctuary Graphic Arts

Printed in the United States of America

Additional copies available from:

www.riversanctuarypublishing.com
amazon.com

River Sanctuary Publishing
P.O Box 1561
Felton, CA 95018
www.riversanctuarypublishing.com

Dedicated to the awakening of the New Earth

Acknowledgments

A big thank you to my family, to my fellow creators in Ron Lampi's group and to everyone at the White Raven in Felton, California.

To all those lovely humans who have entrusted their home and beloved pets to my care: blessings and gratitude to you for allowing me to include my stories about them here.

Last but not least, Annie, David and Melanie at River Sanctuary Publishing for their much appreciated friendship and expertise.

Contents

PART TWO — HEALING ADVENTURES or "Who Heals Whom?"

PART THREE — "I Know These Are Not Cats" TALES OF OTHER ASTOUNDING BEINGS

PART ONE

I Could Have a Cat Now . . .

Little Piece of Heaven

How It All Began

I remember a walk with my dad and my sister on a cold wintry morning many years ago. A little grey kitten came running out to me from the trees. Bending down to pick it up, I was in heaven holding and cuddling it for a while. I had always wanted a cat; it had been a dream as long as I could remember!

Unfortunately, we already were a large family and pets were not allowed at home, which is why in the end my dad chased it off. Our family was run on very authoritarian principles – parents' decisions only – and I had absolutely no say in it. It could also be that my dad was very aware of what my mom's response would be if he brought back her cat-crazy daughter with an actual kitten.

At the time, I could only force myself not to think about what would happen to that tiny little thing in the cold and the snow. Still, even now, after so many years have gone by, whenever I think about it I hope that someone else found it, someone who was able to give it a good home, where it could not just survive but thrive and enjoy life in a loving family with as many cuddles as its little heart could possibly desire.

Fast forward a good few decades . . . In the wake of a relationship breakup, I was again starting anew. It was a huge, exciting project, running a backpackers' hostel and retreat in a big Victorian farmhouse-cum-mansion, something I had never done before, especially not on my own. There was a lot of ground around the house, peacocks were running free, and after a couple of months the thought suddenly appeared, unexpectedly: *'I could have a cat now . . .'*

Famous last words! No sooner had I had the thought an email arrived. Someone wanted to re-home two cats, a mother and nine week old son. *'Oh well, I thought, surely two will be as easy as one, and they can keep each other company.'* and *'It won't hurt to go and have a look . . . I don't have to take them . . .'*

More famous last words! I went to have a look, stroked their heads and backs, said "There, there!" and an hour later I was loading cat mother, kitten and assorted cat paraphernalia into my car. To be honest, I really don't know why they allowed me to take them with me as my inexperience must have been blatantly obvious.

Oh my, what have I done, I thought on the way home. *I know nothing about cats, only that I love them . . . that's not much to go by . . . !*

Back at home I put cushions, beds and things in the workshop, which was really the old servants' kitchen. I had decided that they would live there, and sometimes, when it suited me, I would let them come through into the nice part of the house with me.

Told you I knew nothing about cats!

My new housemates had lovely soft seats, toys that they were used to, food and fresh water – anything I could think of to keep them happy and well. Having reassured myself that everything was fine and dandy I made my way back through to the big room that was my own living space to sit down and ponder this, my latest stroke of genius.

It did feel a bit odd though. Somehow I couldn't really settle that evening. Every half hour or so I got up and went through to the old kitchen to see how they were doing. There they were, Pebbles, the mommy, with lovely dark grey fur, and Brodie the son, grey and white, with a splodge on his nose, both so soft and silky that keeping my hands off them was actually quite hard.

I am not sure what did it in the end, perhaps Pebbles looking at me with her quiet *'What's happening to us?'* look, or Brodie with that little sheepish expression that even now he still shows on occasion. Whatever it was, sometime later that evening I picked up their cushions and beds and brought them through to where I was. They had wrapped me round their soft silky paws the very first night.

By the way, it took me a good two years, I think, until the coin dropped and I realized that Pebbles would have once been a little grey kitten. So, there, the tiny wee thing found its way to me in the end.

Matriarch in the making

It was just *meant* to be because after all these years she was still sitting in a corner of my heart waiting patiently for the right moment to show up.

Because that's what cats do – *I know this much by now.*

Brodie in 'classic sheepish'

Pommie

As you may be able to imagine, my fast track training in *'How To Be A Proper Cat Mom,'* devised and executed by Pebbles and Brodie, was intense. It gave me a good insight into the majority of the pitfalls and insecurities of my new role, but undeterred I was fast becoming much more than just an *afficionado* of the cat world.

One day, only a few weeks after introducing my new furry companions into the household I got a feeling that there was something strange about Pebbles. It was like she was getting fatter. *No,* I thought, *that doesn't make sense. I don't think I am feeding her too much, am I?* And then it was odd, some days it seemed like she was old Pebbles, and on others there appeared a definite 'bulge', But, you've guessed it, she just kept adding to it until eventually there was no mistaking it: Pebbles was neither fat, nor fluffy – she was pregnant, and had been already when I got her.

A few weeks after that realization, in early August, I had visitors. My nephew Mark and three of his friends came for a Scotland tour on their bikes. They weren't too bothered that the weather was not ideal at the time they arrived, but on the day they were planning to leave again it poured and poured, too much to set off in it.

It was an odd morning. After having breakfast, packing and checking their bikes Mark and the guys were kind of restless, wanting to head off into new sights and exciting adventures. Even I was feeling quite unsettled. That's probably why I didn't really notice anything unusual until one of them, Oli, pointed out that Pebbles was behaving strangely.

"I think she's looking for a nest."

"*A nest . . . ?*" I asked, incredulous.

"Yes," he confirmed. "I think she's about to have her kittens."

Birth time! *But I have no clue what to do!*

"It's okay," Oli said. "I grew up on a farm and have seen it many times. Just get her a box and make sure she's comfortable and warm, not too bright. She'll take care of the rest. Trust me, she'll know what to do."

Pebbles and Pommie: Kitten Happy Place

I did as I was told, and in the course of the morning and afternoon, four gorgeous kittens were born. I watched in amazement as, barely born, they went on straightaway to perform a miracle – turning four taciturn young bikers into beaming surrogate dads.

There is a saying that we are only ever given as much as we can handle, and that may have been the case here as well, in the fact that only one of the kittens survived because Pebbles rejected the other three. The one that made it was a cute little black and white thing that we called Poma – which was all of our initials put together in one word. Eventually that became Pomita as a nickname, and then *Pommie* (any connection to Australia unintentional).

I soon learned that knowing a kitten from the moment it is born is another wholly different ball game again. Not only was it a joy to see what a wonderful mom Pebbles was, but also that Brodie, who hadn't been very impressed in the beginning, eventually found a great play mate in Pommie. It was amazing to see how quickly she learned to make use of anything in her surroundings.

Safe Space! "Na na na na nah na..."

A great favorite was playing chase with Brodie and when she needed a rest she'd run for cover under a little rattan book shelf that had a circular ornament at the bottom where Brodie couldn't follow because he had grown too big. Then she'd sit inside her 'safe spot' looking out at him with a teasing gleam in her eyes, daring him to follow.

Before Pommie, I had never had the chance to observe and laugh about the usual kitten activities like chasing her own tail or doing trapeze stunts and such like. And not just that. Her mom Pebbles kept me 'entertained', too. One day, for example, I came home to find an empty nest, something that frightened me no end until I realized that that's what they do after a week or two to keep them safe. It took me a good half an hour's searching to find her in the linen cupboard with Pommie hiding behind some old foam cushions. What a relief!

From a sweet little cute kitten, Pommie grew up into a rather elegant tuxedo 'cabaret cat' with the black mask coming down past her eyes, a black hat and white gloves going up above the 'elbows'. All that was missing was a bow tie and she would have been serious competition for Liza! (I am sure we could have done something about the singing . . .)

Her little pa-*rram*, pa-*rram*, pa-*rram*, pa-*rram*, coming down the stairs greeted me when I came through the front door and was one of the most delightful events of my day.

There were times when she didn't make it quite so gentle though. I remember an evening, when I discovered water leaking down from the upstairs bathroom. It was a Friday night, of course, no tradesmen to be found, and I was running around the house in a panic, trying to suss out what was going on and how to fix it. That involved going up to the attic a few times. To make that easier I wedged open the door to the walk-in linen cupboard that gave access to the attic ladder.

My panic was building because I wasn't getting anywhere. After once again bursting through the door to run up for another useless check upstairs, all of a sudden a great black and white monster leapt down onto me, claws and all. I shrieked at the top of my voice before I figured it was only Pommie and she shot off, down the stairs into hiding. *What on earth was going on?*

In the end my helpful friend Roddy managed to sort out the leak to my big relief leaving me at leisure to attend to the pretty decent scratch right across my forearm that Pommie had given me.

Up for breaking some hearts . . .

Afterwards I pieced together that she must have been sitting on top of the open door – I now know that that's something my cats liked to do on occasion. She must have been agitated, picking up on my stress levels that were going through the roof and her message was something like *'What's got into you, you're behaving like some crazy woman!'* and eventually, when that didn't get me back to my senses: *'I better help sort this out through shock therapy because I don't think anything else will get through!'*

So she pounced on me as if to say, *'Stop this madness!'*

She had a point, of course, and now I have the scar to prove it: *Stress is bad for you!*

OH NO, NOT AGAIN ! . . .

As I have mentioned before, living with cats was a steep learning curve for me, but it would probably be closer to the truth to say that they completely and utterly turned my life upside down.

I really hadn't cottoned on how quickly cats 'move'. It's almost like as soon as one pregnancy is done they can't wait to go and repeat the whole thing: By early October, when Pommie was only a couple of months old, I was shocked to find Pebbles was busy 'cooking up something' – again!

Around that time, a young man, Adrian, came to stay at the hostel for a while. He was an architect and was looking to buy himself a little MG sports car. Early November he found one he liked and asked me would I go to Glasgow with him to pick it up. I would get to drive it back too.

Of course I would, I loved going on adventures!

Therefore, that Saturday we headed off on the early bus *(very early bus)* to Glasgow, picked up the car and with a little detour arrived back home again just before eight.

When I went upstairs I found Pebbles lying on the landing. I bent down to say hello and to stroke her. She looked up at me with a funny expression and said, *"Ph . . . ph . . . ph . . . ph . . !"*

Uh-oh . . . ! Her tummy was heaving and there was only one explanation – poor Pebbles had been lying there waiting for us to come home!

"A-tten-shunnn!"

Thankfully enough, we were back now, everything was ok, so she got up and wobbled to my bedroom as fast as she could manage, me rushing after her. Once arrived, she jumped on my bed – how did she do that . . . ? – and proceeded to give birth on my best llama blanket. Sure, Pebbelie! Only the best for you and your babies! Out they came like clockwork, one every 30 minutes, five of them. Within two and a half hours it was all done and dusted, or rather, *licked.*

It turned out to be a very cold winter that year. One thing that

will stay with me forever is sitting wrapped in a blanket in my cozy chair, reading or chatting and having furry little fluff-balls in every fold of my blanket so that at times I couldn't even lean back for fear of squishing the ones that were snuggled around my neck.

All her fault!

PS Even though I was utterly in love and delighted with these kitties, it was definitely getting a bit crowded in the house by then, as spacious as it was. That's why after this last birth I kept saying to Pebbles, *"Please, please, could you give it a rest now? Could you not have any more kittens for the time being please?"*

Pebbles was great. She listened to my request.

Pommie . . . *didn't.*

Pebbles snooz'n

Tiny

Tiny was one of the grey ones from the litter in early November, the smallest, as the name suggests. Like most of her siblings she was supposed to leave us after New Year's to go to a new, loving home. The friend who had said she wanted her changed her mind though, and somehow I missed the boat finding another place. Therefore, almost by default, Tiny stayed.

She was a very funny kitten, and totally adorable. Everyone loved her, but it still took me a while to notice what an irresistible purr she had.

"Ah di'n't eat it... honess!"

Other cats I have known would start purring once they got into the swing of being cuddled and petted. Not so Tiny. She would see the hand moving towards her and instantly her purr would be turned on in happy anticipation of what was to come. We had very long cuddles together with her leaning and cradling into my hands like none of the others before her.

A favorite habit of hers was to leap onto my shoulder and then walk back down the other arm where she'd jump off. Sometimes she would stay and snuggle up to my ear. I would then walk around with her sitting on me, which made me stoop a little to keep her from falling off. After a while I got to thinking that that must have been one reason why old hags acquired hunchbacks and eventually got called witches . . .

The realization that I was well on my way to that stage wasn't far behind . . . !

Cats are healers. This one is practicing hypnotherapy.

One of my favorites stories about how special she was happened one lovely summer night when I was sitting outside and the cats were out as well, playing their intriguing games of *hide and attack* around me. I took a quick check to see, who was there; all of them – no, Tiny was missing.

"Hm," I thought. *"I wish I knew where Tiny is . . ."*

It didn't take two minutes before she came trundling along the drive towards me, walked right up to my legs and nudged me with her nose, as if to say, *"Now you know!"*

Following that, obviously pleased with herself, she walked right off again.

Another entertaining characteristic – especially for me – was that Tiny spent most of her time outside. She would often just come in for a quick bite and then head off again. In the summer it was frequently very late at night before I got her in.

She didn't come in by herself though. Oh no, not Tiny . . . I regularly had to go out with my flashlight to get her, which was quick sometimes and sometimes it took a bit more effort.

One night I realized that some of the *'rustling flurry'* sounded different from usual. It was a bit odd, and actually took me quite a few days to figure out that that particular sound was caused by a little grey cat crashing down from of her favorite tree, a lone redwood on the lower drive, at top speed – once she thought I had called her enough!

When she eventually responded to my call she startled all the wood pigeons that were roosting there, making them fly off in disgust at the disturbance, which in turn gave me the fright of my life *every time* with the noise they were making . . .

I'm just a little kitten too! No one will notice, right . . .?

Tiny had a generous spirit, and therefore she was delighted when Chouchou and her siblings were born. Her attitude was that she would make the very best of it by having another go at being a kitten, probably with more than one thought of all the delicious perks that came with that . . . because – surely – there was enough for everyone, right?

THE "MOST PERFECTEST" OF CATS . . .

She was a tiny little black kitten in a litter of six. She was very vocal, much more so than her siblings, and her continuous '*feep, feep*' eventually became the name that stuck. I didn't have the heart to call her 'Feep' though, that would have felt too cruel, so I spelled it 'Pheop' in honor of the Old Egyptians because they *really knew* about cats.

"Man, it's crowded in here!"

In the beginning I really didn't have much of a clue what the various feeps meant but one thing became clear quite quickly – a lot of them conveyed something like '*You can give all of the others away but I'm staying right here with you! Did you get that?*'

Peek-a-Boo!

And so she stayed. After all, who could resist such a gentle invitation??

Pheop often used to snooze in the crook of my neck. Yes, I know, you shouldn't let them, they get used to it and you regret it once they reach

Kitty Snooze!

their full weight of half a bag of potatoes . . . but that just didn't come into the equation with her. And so, as she kept growing, she would move further down, to the 'balcony' at first until eventually she stretched from my chin to my hips. One day she must have really cottoned on to the different feel of it. Standing towering above my face, she looked down at me as if to say 'My, you have *shrunk!*'

One of her most endearing traits was that she was always talking to me. Her thrilling little feeps came in all kinds of intonations and with a myriad of different meanings. In that little sound she could express all of the delight and excitement of a life full to the brim with adventure and possibilities.

'I was out running through that high grass, when this THING jumped out at me, and it was REALLY dangerous and I ran and ran, but it didn't catch me, and then I came to this MASSIVE tree that I dashed up, and I NEARLY didn't get back down again, and I went round and round and round and it took AGES to get to the ground!'

All that delivered in feeps with barely a pause for breath . . .

One day I was out pruning shrubs when I heard a little feep coming from ahead and a little above, among the leaves. Looking up

I saw her balancing on one of the branches, as if she was stuck. I stretched out my arms only to get the instinctive cat reaction: *Someone's trying to grab you? RETREAT!*

Realizing I had to make it less 'grabby,' I put the end of my loppers on the branch where she was. At first she looked at me quizzically with her head slightly cocked but then it did the trick. Very carefully she started to walk towards me, balancing on the loppers until she reached my arms and shoulders, from where she jumped to the ground.

Phew, I thought, that's sorted, she's safe now, and I was relieved. It had been kind of a fun game to play as well though . . .

Seems like I was not alone in that view because about 30 seconds later I heard a little '*feep*' coming from ahead and a little above, among the leaves . . .

"One more time, mom! *Feeeeep* . . . ?"

BUBU'S BIRTH

Bubu's story really started weeks before her birth. At the time I had seven cats – too many in a way, because with me running a backpackers hostel where people kept coming and going all the time it was not ideal having cats all over the place. And even though I know it is almost impossible to understand, *not every person is a cat lover!*

Look at these paws!

Bubu's mother Chouchou was my little princess. She was mostly white, with a gray hat, bushy tail and so fluffy that most people thought she was a special breed. Her face was that of a little pixie, in short, she was the cutest wee cat I had ever seen. Then one day I realized that there had been a definite increase in her waistline.

"Oh my god, Chouchou ... Are you – ? Uh-oh ... What am I going to do? I have seven cats already and your kittens will be so cute! How could I possibly decide which one to keep?"

That became my mantra over the next few weeks. "How can I possibly decide which one to keep?" I kept asking her that many, many times.

According to my calculations, the birth was going to happen sometime in late November. I was therefore a little bit confused when one Friday morning at the end of October I noticed Chouchou traipsing around the house, going back and forth, snooping about corners and hiding places in the particular way of a soon-to-be kittycat mommy.

"But ... she can't be ..." I thought. "It's got to be almost another four weeks until she's due."

Of course, with cats you can't tell because ... well, for a start, you weren't there, were you ... and also, trust me, the cat *usually knows better*. So, my little princess picked herself a bed, accepted an old duvet with a fresh cover on and sat there, looking just a tiny little bit worried with all the new things going on.

I sat down next to her, petting her and telling her that it was all going to be fine and that she would be a wonderful mommy, just like her own, Pommie, and her grandma Pebbles had been (she came from good stock). A good half hour later, though, nothing was happening, and I was getting nervous. No one was doing my work, of course!

I gently eased myself off and said, "I've got to do some rooms, Chouch. I'll be back soon."

And off I went.

Another half hour later I heard some hefty footsteps coming down the stairs, pa-*ram*, pa-*ram*, pa-*ram*, pa-*rrram*! Then her fluffy head showed up next to my legs, looking up at me with reproachful eyes that were saying quite clearly, *"Are you coming back now? Where are you when I need you?"*

And so I followed her back upstairs where I sat down, petting and reassuring her that she would be a wonderful mommy ... until I got nervous again because my work wasn't getting done ...

This little game went on all day long. Finally, at 11:15 at night, a little grey and white kitten was born. Chouchou took a bit of time to understand the licking and cleaning process but eventually got the hang of it, and the little one came crawling round squeaking to be fed.

For some reason he seemed to have problems finding the teat though. He kept getting close only to lose it again. After a while and increasingly louder squeaks I picked him up and lifted him to the source of the good stuff, but even putting his little mouth right onto it didn't do the trick. The squeaks were getting more and more desperate and still he wouldn't drink.

It seemed like a long time had passed already. My heart was going out to the little fellow but nothing I did seemed to make any difference. Eventually I reminded myself that I had to be calm no matter what. That's when I thought I could try some tapping (Emotional Freedom Technique) to help.

"Chouchou Belle... Service Please!"

I sat up and started tapping *"Even though I am really really hungry but I can't drink, I love and accept myself completely."*

I was on the third round only when I heard some kind of a smacking noise – there he was, suckling like crazy!

Oh, thank God, I thought, this one's sorted. Now, who's next?

I looked at Chouchou, reached out, petted her again, waited for the next contractions. Then I waited some more, and still some more. At a quarter past three in the morning I had almost convinced myself that that was all there was – one kitten. Nothing else in there. I didn't see how, but that's what it looked like.

Just to be on the safe side, I made up a bed for myself opposite hers. She was not totally happy about the constant surveillance, especially not once granny Pebbles joined us too. Too many people in this maternity ward for her taste, that much was clear. I had to sleep there though because I would have not found any rest in my bedroom, worrying if they were alright all night.

But the next morning dawned and everyone was fine. Phew. One kitten only.

Chouchou must have listened well to me when I said, '*how am I going to choose, which one to keep, Chouch? I won't be able to do that because they're all going to be so drop dead gorgeous, how on earth am I going to choose the one to keep . . .*

So now Bubu is a rare 'only kitten' . . . who is still not awfully keen on milk!

Bubu's a Girl?

Naming a kitten is a delightful task and one I very much enjoyed. Of course, it's a highly individual process and you're never quite sure what you're going to come up with in the end.

What an exciting world!

Sometimes they make it easy by showing their characteristics quite quickly, like the little black kitten, for example, who at the age of perhaps seven, eight weeks came across a bowl of mashed potato laced with a serious amount of butter. One lick and she decided it was hers and hers alone. When Brodie staggered in, (about five times her size) she defended her prize against him with not so much as half a nod in his direction and a growl that would have done a fully grown panther proud. After that, there was only one name worthy of her – Bagheera – and truly deserved it was, too.

With Bubu, to be honest, I don't really have a clear idea where the name came from. I had checked the 'bits', found they were male and somehow 'Bubu' came up. It was supposed to be provisional at first, only until I'd come up with something better.

At that particular time I had seven cats and I knew that sooner or later I would have to take Bubu to the vet to get neutered, even though I really didn't want to. After much hesitation I made 'the appointment' and dropped him off. About an hour later, I got a phone call from the vets informing me that my cheeky little boy

Was I born for the camera or what?

Bubu was a girl! (In my defense I would like to point out that I don't go round checking my cats' genitals all the time.)

I think it was when I drove back to the vets' to bring home Bubu girl that I got the first inkling of understanding why her name was perhaps more appropriate than I had initially thought . . .

Being an single kitten meant that Bubu had no siblings to grow up with, which is why it may have been only natural for lovely little black Pheop ('Feep'), who was just three months older, to step in as a nanny, playmate and best friend. The two quickly became inseparable.

Once the weather turned milder, Pheop wanted to go out every minute of the day, so she could enjoy all the exciting sounds and smells everywhere and then rush back and tell me about it in excited feeps full of abounding adventure. Slowly, slowly, I allowed Bubu, who was still quite small then, to join her. They had a whale of a time playing together, making me laugh out loud, especially because Pheop had the *spring lamb jump* (straight up in the air) as well as the sideways *sproingy skip* down to perfection.

One sunny day in mid-March they were again out running and chasing things in the banks along the drive in front of the house.

There were a couple of bushes and shrubs there, a few cotone-aster, but mostly broom. At some point Bubu was sitting at the edge, watching in fascination, looking up at something in the broom. Her tail, still growing and not fully fluffed yet had that odd triangular shape of a kitten's, and it was wagging like a dog's.

Cats have amazing patience when it comes to stalking things. I, however, don't! I was standing there with the camera, hoping to catch whatever exciting thing she was going to do next – but she didn't. Time went past and then a car. I thought, oh well, that's it, false alarm.

Then, just as I was pressing the stop button, Bubu jumped, missed the branch and somersaulted back down onto the grass. It was the only time ever I felt grateful that my camera was so slow to respond because thanks to that I had managed to get most of it except her landing. A pea-hen walking by with her head crest sticking up into the bottom of the picture provided an interest-ing side effect though.

Like every other being, kittens have milestones in their devel-opment. Apparently the cat equivalent of a child grazing their knees for the first time is getting stuck in a tree.

The following day had been lovely and warm but the evening was feeling a bit chilly. I was inside, doing the usual bits of sort-ing things out when I suddenly thought I hadn't seen Bubu for a while. Also, Chouchou was sort of marching back and forth in a funny way.

"Where's little Bubu?" I asked, but she didn't give me any clues. Putting my jacket on, I went outside and walked around the garden calling her. On the second round I heard a little high-pitched noise coming from the trees by the wall. I went closer but still couldn't see anything.

Such a Poser!

"Bubu!" I called. "Where are you, Bubu? I can hear you, but I can't see you!"

Again the desperate little kitten sound *"Eeh! Eeh!"* I looked up and noticed that, despite my assumption that the trees hadn't been pruned in decades, someone had actually done some work up there, leaving a few stumps at about 8 or 9 ft high and on the resulting tiny platform was where Bubu sat crying, almost invisible from below.

By that time Chouchou had found us, too. She sat down by the bottom of the trees and looked at me in that old English country lady way that only she could do.

"She's up on the tree top. What are you going to do about it? She's right up there, all the way. Are you going to do something . . . ? *Eh?*"

It was clearly a ladder job. The wooden step ladder I got first was far too short. I had really known that before but was hoping that somehow I would manage because the other option was threading an aluminum ladder through the branches and I wasn't sure I was going to be able to do that.

Next I tried the single 8 ft ladder, but by the time I had managed to place that one Bubu had changed her position to a platform slightly higher than the one she had occupied before. Whether she got scared and tried to save herself or was making another effort to get down on her own, I couldn't say. I was just hoping it was not because she was having me on . . .

Chouchou was still at the bottom of the trees, pacing back and forth now, looking at me reproachfully for the disappointing speed and process of the rescue operation.

"She's up there. Still all the way up. Are you going to do something useful now?'

The extendable ladder was aluminum, too, but quite a lot longer and heavier than the other one. I staggered through the trees with it and after a number of unsuccessful efforts finally managed to secure it against some branches, sort of. Then I climbed up to where Bubu was.

As soon as she saw me, she shrank back from my arms. Yes, I know . . . someone's trying to grab you – *retreat!*

I went up another rung when the ladder started to wobble and suddenly I had enough. I reached out, no nonsense, grabbed her by the scruff of the neck and did not let go until we were safely back down on the ground.

"There ya go, Chouch! Kitten rescue completed successfully! What are you saying now?"

"Hm," said Chouchou. "very good, I guess." Then she sniffed her paw and said, "What took you so long?", turned and meandered back into the house, on the trail of her little renegade off-spring.

I shrugged and walked back to the house, picking accumulated leaves and bits of trees from all over myself and sighed.

It was clearly time for a cup of tea. Or maybe something stronger than that. . . ?

COMMUNICATION

One of the aspects that fascinates me most about living with cats is seeing the way they make choices, come to conclusions and put their decisions into practice. Chouchou for example would always claim the space in my lap when I was at the computer, while Brodie had made it clear that to the right of me on the sofa was his place in the evening.

"I think it fell..."

At some point I began to suspect that there was more communication possible between us than the usual 'here kitty kitty' kind of exchanges.

There had already been some occasions that were almost startling in their clarity of transmission, like that one time when everyone seemed to be intent on a fight to the death against the *big bad worming pill.*

We were all stressed out and agitated, the house had been turned into a war zone and after Chouchou had managed to escape from my lovingly wrapped towel burrito again – God knows how she did it! – I sat on the floor looking at her, just about at the end of my tether, and exclaimed, *"Why why WHY will you not take this medicine?"*

To which she calmly replied, straight into my mind and with perfect clarity, so as to avoid any doubts whatsoever: *"You don't take any of that stuff yourself. Why should we?"*

I was floored, in every imaginable way. How had she picked up on the fact that I avoided any pharmacological products if at all possible, and more than that, that I actually considered most of them detrimental? It was astounding . . .

That experience had a profound effect on me. First of all it proved to me once and for all that my cats were a lot more than fluffy objects of affection or entertainment and that their lives and activities extended way beyond the generally acknowledged eat, sleep and get petted kind of lifestyle.

It became obvious to me that their learning scope reached further than the location of their food bowl and the paths around the garden, it actually looked like they made pretty abstract decisions about themselves and their lives. I suddenly understood that they were not *mere pets* but rather beings in their own right and should be treated as house mates, to be respected and considered, just like myself.

I had a habit of spending a lot of my time at the computer, not just for work but also for education and enjoyment, and yes, I have to admit there are times when my little netbook even got to go to bed with me. Bubu had adopted the habit of watching for my bedtime and when she'd see me get ready she would jump on the bed to curl up beside me.

One such night I was reading longer than expected because of some fascinating articles on a site I was engrossed in. The words were having a deep effect on me, I felt stimulated and uplifted. At one point my eyes were pulled off the screen and Bubu caught my attention.

She was sitting facing me, slightly to the left, but instead of being curled up snoozing, her little face was resting on the paws that were folded up under her. She was watching me intently.

Looking up at her beautiful features I was bowled over by her adorable cuteness and couldn't take my eyes off her. I was over-flowing with love for this delightful little bundle.

Then Bubu did something I had never seen her do before. She began to move her head almost as if she was tracing a halo around my head and back, again and again, her eyes full of wonder. I looked at her, tears welling up, laughing at the same time.

"Bubu, you little silly! What are you doing . . . ?"

The answer came more as a sense of understanding rather than words: "Watching fireworks . . ."

I burst out laughing. Of course . . . She was looking at my aura where the intensity of the love and joy I was feeling must have set in motion a light show like she had never seen before!

At that moment something else occurred to me. Time for an experiment . . . I looked straight at Bubu and very intently formed the following thought as a message while at the same time put-ting my hand palm up in front of her: "Bubu, if you can 'hear' this, put your paw in my hand."

Then I waited to see what would happen.

I had to repeat it a couple of times but then, quick as lightning, her paw reached out, touched my palm and was gone again.

I blinked. Did that really happen? I thought I was pretty sure but the moment had been so brief I also had doubts. Could be wishful thinking . . . ?

"Okay," I thought, again directed at her. "That was so fast, I didn't really get it. Could you do it again please?"

This time I totally felt her resistance. She was Wild Junior Princess Kitty and not here to be used as a lab rat or performing monkey! *How slow can those humans be...? I mean, d'uh...!*

But Bubu loved me as much as I loved her and so again, the extraordinary happened . . . Her paw quickly tapped my palm and this time round, as soon as it was done, with the grace of a ballet dancer she changed into position for a grooming session . . .

"Oh, sorry, did I hit you there . . ? I just needed to stretch for my night time bath..."

I laughed at this complete denial of her acquiescence but I also had to admire the spunk and attitude in that little ball of fur.

Wanna clean up this mess now?

Family Dynamics

Can I help you?

Where more than one cat share life in the same house there is always something going on . . . If you asked them, they would probably call it entertainment!

Recently I had been noticing that, despite being really streetwise, Tiny was getting more and more timid. She had stopped coming into my bed at night and I wasn't quite sure whether that was because Chouchou had spent a few nights with me or whether Bubu's 'sphinx position' on my bed as guardian of the bedroom put her off.

I had also seen Chouchou and Tiny chasing each other on occasion but could never quite make out who started it. The only option I felt I had there was to adopt the 'mother position' that said, *'I don't care who started it – both of you: stop now!'*

One night I was preparing a room quite late when Tiny came in. She had been following me on and off, doing that restless bit for a while, where I never quite know if she wants to find a cozy place or just be around me.

She didn't seem too keen on cuddles though so I went about my business making beds and sorting things out for the next day. But when Brodie came swaggering in Tiny instantly changed, suddenly showing signs of nervousness. He noticed and headed straight towards her but I quickly realized what he was up to.

Stepping in his path, I stopped him from getting to her. He walked to the left, found me in front of him again, went back to the right – same thing. He looked up at me in surprise, the question of *'What on earth are you doing?'* in his eyes.

I didn't want to make him nervous as well and perhaps end up getting him frightened of me, so after a few of these exchanges I simply walked over and picked him up. That was even more of a surprise! He held still as I carried him to the door of his favorite room. The window there was open, which meant he could snuggle up inside or go out, whichever he preferred. I let him down – just as well because he was starting to get restless – and then I left, shutting the door behind me.

Back in the other room I gave Tiny a good reassuring cuddle and finished off the room. There, now I was all ready to put my feet up.

There is never a long period of sitting down with multiple cats though, and not long after that, when I had to let Bubu out I noticed Brodie passing by outside. Thinking he might want to come back in I tapped on the window to let him know I was there to open it again, but he had already gone from sight.

Gonna getcha!

I went into the hall only to find myself opposite him. He obviously had come in through the back door. In his mouth was a big scrumptious mouse – well, I guess, 'scrumptious' is a matter of opinion, I'm sure.

He plonked it down, then, looking up at me expectantly, gave a little meow.

'I got this just for you. I do hope you will enjoy it . . .'

He really deserved some 'proud Mom praise and strokes' for that, which he received promptly . . . Then I went and made the mouse disappear out the back.

Thankfully cats accept things quickly. After snooping around the rug for a bit he came to the conclusion that the mouse had vanished and there was no point crying over it. So he didn't.

After all, there was always his nice, soft sleeping place.

You take my mouse, I give you the
cold shoulder!

Stranger In a Pub, or "This One's Got a Sister!"

It was a 'round birthday' weekend in late September a few years ago. My sister had come to visit, and also my brother and his girlfriend. The day of the party had been wonderful – blue skies, sunny, and quite warm for the season, but the rest of the weekend was abysmal. Scotland was showing itself from its most stereotypical side, wet and grey, no views – pretty much whisky weather!

My brother and his girlfriend were due to leave on Tuesday, which meant that by Monday I felt the urgency of the situation and that drastic action on my part was required.

Skye: Next time you can see the top half too!

"Let's get out of here!" I said.

The reply I received was less than enthusiastic. "Where do you want to go in this miserable weather?"

"Anywhere! We have to get out and do something . . . "

"But you can't even see anything . . . !"

I hadn't had ten years as a tour guide for nothing so my cheerful reply came quite naturally: "In that case, you can see a totally different country when you're here next – you'll see the top half as well . . . I hope . . . !"

Thankfully my professional charm did the trick. We all packed into my brother's beautiful brand new rental Volkswagen Passat, and headed off to the Isle of Skye. The coffee shop on the way was closed, bad luck, but the first couple of viewpoints were reasonable, which on that day translated to not overly uncomfortable to get out and admire the scenery.

On Skye itself we were not quite as lucky. Lunch was a picnic in the car in a very rainy car park at Broadford Bay. Despite the novelty value I have to admit that even my enthusiasm was slightly affected, which was possibly the reason why on the road back to Kyle I suddenly had a crazy idea.

"Would anyone be interested in something really special?"

The question was met with what could only be called suspicious caution. I suppose they knew what kind of suggestions to expect from me by then.

"What did you have in my mind . . . ?"

"Well, there is this ferry that goes from Kylerhea to Glenelg. It's been running for about 900 years – no, relax, it's not the original

Four Ws: Wet & Windy means Whisky Weather!

one any more – and has recently, last year, I believe, been taken over by the community. It takes about ten cars and used to have a ferry dog, a collie that would inspect everything before they'd cast off . . ."

I don't know how it happened but they actually agreed to my hare-brained idea and so we headed up into the rain-swept and windy roads of Glen Arron. I had told them that it was a very interesting drive but they possibly did not realize at the time that that meant a tiny single track road, extremely windy, and not just sideways but also up and down.

In my defense it has to be said that even on a rainy day it is a fairly spectacular drive, just because of how steep the roads are there and the breathtaking vistas at just about every turn. After some exceedingly interesting curves where it always looked like the road was going to disappear into nothing we came down the hill and round the last bend towards the ferry point.

I got ready to drive on, directed by one of the ferry crew. There were all new faces at the ferry, and because I was very curious about how the recent community takeover had worked out for them I had a lot of questions to ask. My brother obviously hadn't realized that I had become quite the 'chatting to strangers person' and was suitably impressed. "Man," he said with his usual side to side smirk, "she talks to just about everybody!"

The crossing from Kylerhea to Glenelg is quite short but always enjoyable, not just for the seals and sea birds that kept us fascinated but also the views onto the surrounding mountains. By the time we were driving off the vessel at the other end we all felt quite pleased with the experience and everyone perked up a little.

Grateful for the uplifting change that had happened since our ferry ride I happily navigated the tiny roads towards Glenelg, when my eyes caught sight of a sign that said *Glenelg Inn*. It looked brand new and very attractive. I could have sworn it had never been quite so nice and shiny before . . .

Hm . . . I thought, and straightaway blurted out my latest idea: "Does anyone fancy a visit to the pub? There is one right here I have never yet been able to get to . . . "

It was half past three in the afternoon on a Monday. My brother thought that was a perfectly fine time to go to the pub. Since neither his girlfriend nor my sister objected, I pulled into the car park and we went right in.

Once inside, the first thing I noticed was a tabby cat curled up in a chair sleeping peacefully. The second was that there was hardly any one else there. One guy at the bar, one behind the bar, that was it. Well, it was a Monday afternoon and so far our day had not exactly been fireworks. What the heck, we thought, and proceeded to order drinks.

The Glenelg Inn used to have a reputation for live music, something I was always keen on, and which had to be checked out. I therefore began asking the barman questions about it. The other guy, an Irishman, joined in the conversation and soon enough we had some slightly surreal but hilarious banter going. It turned out that the Irishman was actually the pub landlord.

Ah, in that case, I had to ask, of course: "Is that your cat that's curled up so nicely over there?"

"He came with the pub . . . Do you want to take a picture? Here, come with me, take a picture!" and before I knew it he was storming off across the bar room, motioning me and my camera to follow.

At first the pub cat didn't show that much of an interest, to be honest, but he was a lovely boy anyway. I accepted the invitation to take a picture, so as not to be rude. I have to apologize

Could this cool dude be interested?

for the poor quality of it though. It just felt wrong to traumatize the poor sleepy thing with flash photography.

Meantime the others had noticed that the action had moved away from the bar a bit and had wandered over to see what was going on.

I pulled my cell phone out and said, "I have cats too, look…" showing the pub owner my screen saver, which was a picture of fluffy white gorgeous Mu-ki. "Isn't she a beauty?"

Before I could say another word he had grabbed the phone out of my hand and was holding it in front of the cat's face.

"Hey, look here . . . " he said. "She's nice, isn't she?"

Mu-Ki: Angel Kitty in the Snow

I was completely taken by surprise. The last thing I had expected here was a cat dating service and not wanting to lead anyone on, I said "Oh, I'm sorry . . . she's no longer with us . . . She got run over this summer, poor wee thing . . . "

He handed me the phone back instantly, obviously anxious not to get his boy's hopes up.

At that point I felt that I should do something to keep the disappointment at bay. I therefore added quickly "She's got a lovely sister though, looks quite similar, called Chouchou . . . "

He snatched the phone back again, held it in front of the cat's face once more, and with a voice full of persuasion and seductive promise announced "This one's got a sister . . . "

By that time we were all in hysterics and I was still laughing my socks off as I drove the car back onto the main road heading for home.

There's always a party somewhere in Scotland even on a rainy Monday afternoon – if it's only for cat matchmaking purposes . . .

Mu-ki: Superior Level Agent

Gingey-Morgan (Garfield)

Gingey-Morgan Master Patience Player Who'd'a thunk? (Photo: Kes Rose)

I suppose you could be forgiven for saying that it was 'just my luck' to move into a rambling, single glazed, drafty Victorian house just before we were hit with some of the worst winters in recent history.

Whatever the reasons were that brought me there and whatever take you might have on it, it certainly made me very aware of what other creatures might be going through.

That's probably why when I saw that skinny little ginger fellow hover around my drive in the deep snow my heart went out to him, and I more or less instantly made the reckless mistake of feeding him. I didn't know the old rule then (*'You feed them, you keep them . . .'*).

He was quite shy at the time and it took me a while to gain his trust. That didn't bother me too much, though, as I already had a few cats, and despite the fact that he was cute, I didn't really want another one.

Over the following weeks things fell into a rhythm. He would come for a bite and then head off again on his wanderings, which made me assume that he had a number of feeding stations at least, apparently was streetwise and well capable of fending for himself.

After a few weeks though, I had a feeling I should make some enquiries. Through the local cats protection league branch I managed to find Gingey's people, and one day shortly after that

Making cute...

an elderly man brought a teenage girl for a tearful reunion with the cat I then found out was called 'Garfield.'

Relieved that all had come to a good end, I said my goodbyes and waved them off, Garfield cuddled by his little miss on the front seat, and that was that.

Or so I thought!

It wasn't much more than a week or so later, guess who came trundling up my drive, sweet and innocent as can be? No other than Mr Gingey-Garfield!

The next few months saw pretty frequent repeats of the following events or very similar ones at least: Garfield showing up, phone call to elderly gentleman (grandpa), arrival of vehicle, looking for Garfield (where is he now?) and a drive back home.

For reasons I didn't understand at the time, this got tiring for Garfield's family. Though it was never said openly, I began to suspect it from the more and more lukewarm responses I received when I rang them. Over time I found out where they lived, which in turn changed the schedule of events to something like this: Arrival at the house. Nice bit of dinner. Cat gets packed into my car to be chauffered home.

I have to say that Garfield was so easy in the car that I stopped using a carrier more or less straight away. He would either walk around trying to look out the window or he would stand with his front legs on the dashboard, following the road and all the exciting things that went on outside. Sometimes he would even curl up peacefully on my lap. His absolute favorite was to look out of the window though.

In the meantime spring had turned to summer. More changes were in the air. There were days when I took Garfield home around lunch time only to find he was back, meowing outside my bedroom window by 2am! And then, more and more I thought I noticed a certain reluctance in him to get out of my car at home and leave.

Most of the times I dropped him by his family's house he didn't look back at me, but on occasion he just stood there, as if trying to psyche himself up for going where he felt he didn't belong any more. This was confirmed by a friend who had heard that by then he was regarded as 'just another mouth to feed'.

I was pretty clear that I couldn't keep him myself. At that time not all of my cats had been neutered yet and to introduce a new member, who was not even of the same family seemed inadvisable. So I started to look for another home for him.

I soon found a young family, who seemed absolutely delighted to have him. I was under a lot of pressure at the time – the summer season was in full swing with the house full of guests – and therefore I suppose might be forgiven for not being quite as careful as I should have been.

The fact that I sent Garfield into a similar situation that he had been trying to escape from was brought back to me after about two weeks when I finally found time to call the new family. I was sorry to hear it wasn't going so well and my offer of taking him back immediately was met with unconcealed relief. When they brought him back my heart sank at the look of him. His personality had changed visibly. He was nowhere near as bolshy as he had been before and felt smaller somehow. I was shocked and full of remorse wondering about what could have traumatized him so in that short space of time.

So I took him in for another round . . . This time he got a bed in the workshop as the season turned into winter and he was quite happy to eat the leftovers from the others along with some dry food.

All was reasonably well for a while, though on occasion he and Brodie would give 'concerts' together. I liked the howling of the cats but it wasn't always good when there were guests around, as cats don't seem to have a lot of respect or understanding for a human's need to sleep. Also, knowing that the concerts were actually confrontations and show offs did spoil my listening fun a little bit.

Another spring came round and with the days getting longer and warmer I had doors and windows open as much as I could. Somehow that created an opening in another way for Gingey-Garfield. It was as if he saw it as an invitation to come and explore the house, which soon yielded some interesting results. For one, he suddenly realized that there was a lot better food to be had than everyone else's leftovers, and secondly, and a lot more important, that there was a much better sleeping place to be had than the one in the workshop – and this prime location was, of course, *my bed!*

Obviously again, he owed it to himself, as the prime cat, for that's how he saw himself, to go straight for the conquest.

You can see that Gingey was a resilient fellow, who had recuperated well from his ordeal in the thuggish housing project I had sent him to in my carelessness. Actually, I was beginning to fear that he might even have picked up a few new tricks that he was now putting to good use on my soft, harmless and pretty spoilt bunch.

More and more he was seen wondering through the house, using his tiny little 'elbows' bit by bit, sometimes a little more than others, until eventually he had established himself on my bed, successfully outing Matriarch Pebbles as well as Chouchou, the lovely fluffy white and anthracite princess.

I have to say that I often found myself thinking that I didn't appreciate his methods and I also began to suspect that he was separating me from the others but I was too busy for a closer investigation.

One warm night in the summer, the end of a hard and very busy working day, everything changed though. It was getting late and I was absolutely exhausted, wanting to go to bed as soon as possible. I set about making sure everyone was fine, locked up the chickens and checked to see which of the cats needed 'herding' in.

Opening the back door to my kitchen I was pleased to see Brodie and Pebbles running up to come inside. What I didn't realize was that Gingey had sneaked up behind me and was threatening them, chasing them away from behind my back, making them turn and bounce right off again, back outside.

I turned around, saw him standing there, hackles up, completely domineering, and my heart broke at the realization and the thoughts that came with it: *"You're OUT!"*

An hour later I was on the computer emailing the local Cats Protection branch to see if they had a space for him. They didn't, but they were willing to put him up on their website with a couple of photographs.

What happened then was nothing short of a miracle.

It must have been almost to the minute when Gingey chased off my cats and got my marching orders that a short distance away a family lost their beloved cat, *a ginger tom*.

Everyone who has ever shared their life with a pet knows they can't be replaced like a sweater, and yet, sometimes taking in another one straight away is the perfect thing to do.

The next day or so the woman was online, found Gingey's picture, knew at once that it was him she wanted and got in touch. We agreed that she could come to see him almost immediately.

I was at my favorite coffee shop when the call came in.

Being Santa is an exhausting job
(Photo: Kes Rose)

I rushed home to get him in, as Gingey loved to be outside and I felt I should have him in the house by the time she arrived.

I found him but noticed to my horror that he was filthy! He had always been a bit grubby but God knows what he had been doing precisely on that afternoon; there was no way I could present him like that!

It was a tough decision – and a first for me – but Gingey was going to get a bath . . .

I lined the upstairs bathroom with old towels and sheets and walked up with him cradled in my arms. By the time he realized it was not just a mammoth cuddling session I was already putting the cat soap on him.

Then, however, the events changed from peaceful and happy to big drama. He would struggle out of my grip, claw his way up my shoulder and then jump onto the floor, only to be picked up again and have the procedure repeated until he was done, or rather, we both were!

The bathroom, including myself, was flooded, he was soaking wet and really annoyed, and I needed a shower myself. First though, I wrapped him in a big towel and plonked him on my bed.

This time he had absolutely *no* gratitude whatsoever for the privileged position and every attempt at reconciliation was met with a cold glare and an indignant "Can't you see I'm busy licking myself dry? Some idiot thought I should have a bath!"

According to the agreed appointment I had just a little under two hours to get Gingey presentable before his potential new family arrived.

I should have known though that they wouldn't be able to wait . . . I don't think I would have managed, either.

A good hour before the time a car pulled up and there they were at the door. I went to fetch Gingey downstairs where we all sat down to talk.

Perhaps due to the fact that he was still a bit wet he looked quite sweet and almost vulnerable wrapped in his towel. After his bath ordeal he may have actually felt like that, and perhaps even a bit sorry for himself, too . . . Despite it being a lovely sunny day, he somehow hadn't warmed up at all, and so he was picked up and cuddled dry, smothered in love from the minute they set eyes on each other.

Gingey is now King of the Castle and every so often these days I get emails from his new family. He is now called Morgan because he purrs like a beautiful expensive car.

PS I am told that inside the house he is an angel but whenever he gets out he becomes his old thug-self, scaring the life out of the neighbor's big dog.

Oops.

Sorry, doggie!

SUPERKITTY

Crackers: Nothing gets past me!

This particular kitten came from the precious line of Pebbles' offspring. He was solid grey, like a lot of her babies and didn't stand out much in the beginning. Behind his male kitten 'me, me me' attitude there was also something sweet about him. Seeing as he was crazy about milk I felt seriously tempted to call him 'Cadbury' because he was a 'dairy nut.' In the end, being the chocolate snob that I am, I couldn't bring myself to name this cute boy after what I considered inferior quality chocolate, so he stayed 'kitty boy' for quite a while.

We had been having a fine summer and one night I took the opportunity to have a bonfire in the garden with our guests. The party went on for quite a while, it was almost midnight when I finally got to bed. I was dog tired but took a plastic tub with the remaining crackers up to my room. After a good night's sleep the sun woke me up in the morning along with a funny sound that I couldn't place. Something was making a crunching noise, 'k-rk, k-rk, k-rk . . .'

I sat up and looked around me. By the side of my bed on the floor was the tub of crackers I hadn't finished before falling asleep. Inside it was a grey kitty, munching away like a champion! "K-rk, k-rk, k-rk . . .!"

"That's it," I thought. "You're Crackers!"

He didn't stop at this odd kind of behavior either. Watching Chouchou sidle up to lick the butter off my toast at breakfast time didn't impress him all that much, but it sure gave him ideas.

"Look, mom, *I* can eat the bread as well!"

Very soon I felt it was time to expand his name because the old one just wasn't saying it properly. This kitty ate ham, toast, olives and even pine nuts! He was pretty classy about his food . . . perhaps a touch Italian? And when he showed up again after being missing for over a day he ate broccoli soup offered by caring hostel guest Lara from Australia, who thankfully enough was eating her lunch out in the sun when he finally made it back home.

In the end his full 'official' name with more than a cheeky nod to breeders was 'Crackers Antipasto Caruso, *The Ham-ster*'. Caruso was well-deserved because I had never had the pleasure of being serenaded by any of the others cats the way he would go on when he saw me get the packet of ham from the fridge.

Crackers had another, bigger adventure though, beyond his fancy name and culinary preferences. I came out of the kitchen door one morning to find him sitting there all quiet, which was very unusual for him. Watching him with surprise at this behavior I saw blood on his mouth and finally understood that he was injured and needed emergency treatment immediately. The diagnosis didn't sound good, a broken leg and injured jaw from having been hit by a car. The vet didn't give me much hope about being able to save the leg.

They promised me to do what they could to avoid an amputation but when the post surgery call came through I was told it had not been possible. A few days later I was allowed to pick him up, which I did with a heavy heart.

Outside is heaven!

Back at the house I took the carrier with Crackers inside and put it on the floor in the kitchen. Then I opened the door for him to get out. Slowly he understood that he was free to leave his cage.

His movements were quite tentative but got a little more determined with every step. His first destination was the fridge. There's *got to be ham inside . . . ?*

Poor Crackers looked like Hannibal Lecter! I had not realized how much his mouth had been smashed up in the accident. With his jaw full of wires he wasn't able to eat the ham. My heart was bleeding for him. Now what . . .

But Crackers would not have been Crackers if he had let this bring him down. Next stop, the garden! The vet had told me in no uncertain terms "Do not let him out for at least two days!" but he didn't know Crackers the way I did. He couldn't eat, what else could I offer him . . ?

Step by tiny baby step we walked all the way down the length of the house to the back of the extensive garden with him leading the way. It was like a mindfulness meditation for the sake of my kitty boy who was now learning how to walk again with his front leg missing. He was a marvel to watch. His patience, his determination and his delight about being out of the steel cage, finally back among his trees and flowers again were as palpable as if I was experiencing it myself.

We kept going, past the living room windows, the fragrant hedge underneath them and he didn't stop at the edge of the fruit trees either. All the way to the back he went, where the garden became wild and turned into woodlands full of fairy scent. There by the big pine trees among the mosses he stopped . . . and took a big dump!

Oh Crackers, *you crack me up!* I can so see and feel how wonderful this must have been after spending a week cramped up in a cage surrounded by lifeless steel walls. He looked at me as if he was saying, 'thank you for understanding this important need, to be out again among my trees, in nature, where I belong. Though I have to say I would have preferred a little privacy for this particular activity . . . '

He was ready to go back in again after that and together we began the new and unexpected phase of feeding him. It didn't take me long to find out that he couldn't chew, which meant that I had to find more creative ways to keep him in food. For weeks my kitchen floor look like a Japanese restaurant with me creating an endless variety of dishes for him.

A worried internet search provided some relief because apparently a fair number of cat parents have this issue: "My cat doesn't chew!" I started to experiment with different combinations of food, some with cooked chicken, some with cat milk, some with a little cream, some fish, all blended to ensure minimum necessity for moving his jaw. The first few meals took a long, long time, because in the beginning he could hardly open his mouth and gradually I understood that his tongue was lacerated and the wires in his jaw were hurting him, so everything, even water, had to be given gently and with great care.

We took it really slowly. After a few false starts he was able to lick the purée from my finger, filling me with a wave of joy, and I couldn't stop welling up a little for the hope this gave me. I finally got why the vet had not been awfully troubled by the amputation – they were much more worried about his jaw. Would he be able to eat and keep himself alive through his recovery . . ?

It was a busy time at the hostel, though thankfully not full summer season yet and I had made a point of visiting Crackers at the vets' as often as possible while he was there. I gave him reiki, and much to the credit of the vet they let me bring my color lights to apply on him as well. Perhaps his wonderful spirit was supported enough to keep his faith and his optimism with the treatments.

I had to go about my daily business again but kept checking in on him to make sure he had everything he needed. The hostel was a big house and there were times in the beginning when he frightened me, like when he, true to his cat nature, followed his instinct and crept underneath a unit in my office. It must have taken an hour or more of intense searching to finally discover his hideaway, but I could see his need for a safe, confined nook, even though we had no predators in or around the house.

I gave him the opportunity to heal outside as much as he needed to. Being among the grass and the trees seemed an overriding desire and I trusted his choice and his instinct. I had to keep the times relatively short because I could only take half an hour here and there and I didn't want to exhaust him too much. One day though he was just simply gone and no matter how much I searched and called he never showed up until just before midnight. It was bad for my nerves, I can tell you! And he never even told me where he'd been, that little rascal . . .

When his jaw had healed enough that we could go to the vet and have his wires removed I don't know who was more relieved, him or me. His excitement about eating normal food once more was a delight to watch. Finally he could enjoy his much missed chicken and his ham again.

The world was back in order, *nom nom . . .*

But again, Crackers being Crackers, he had already set his next goal: climb his favorite trees. By the time he had mastered that nothing stopped him any more and eventually he even got back into hunting again.

Hats off to Crackers Antipasto Caruso, The Ham-ster – *SuperKitty*!

Whooaaah... MOM...!!!

THE CAT THAT THOUGHT SHE WAS A COW

This morning I was washing the dishes in the kitchen when Bubu came in. She kept saying 'Me-ooh, me-ooh!' and the following story is about what that did to my head.

I blame Bubu ... (because it couldn't be my head now, could it ...)

A long long time ago there was an adventurous little kitten named T'Beau who had been told so many stories about a magical planet called Earth that it made her want nothing more than to go and see it all.

She wanted to nibble the juicy green grass among colorful and fragrant flowers and play tag with the little feathery things that they said would be fluttering through the air.

T'Beau found the stories so wonderful and enchanting that her desire to go there grew stronger and stronger with every day.

Every night before she went to sleep she would pray, "Oh please, let me go to Earth and see this wondrous planet! I so want to play with all these amazing things and bounce about in the grass that is so green it makes your eyes go funny. I can almost smell the fragrance of the flowers already!"

One night when the tiny little kitten was fast asleep a fierce wind came up. The gales howled and raged, and suddenly T'Beau was up in the air, flying, being blown here and there, up and down, and to every side, so that all she could do was to squinch her eyes tight shut and hope for the best.

When she opened them again, she was stunned by what she saw.

"Wow ..." she said. Everything was so green! And there were the flowers, beautiful and sweet as she had been told. It was really lovely ... and even more than she had imagined.

But hold on . . . over there was a big brown thing – and it was coming towards her!

T'Beau had always been a fearless kitten. At that moment though she wished that someone had told her how big the cats were on Earth, because it was clear to her without a doubt that she had been granted her wish and this was indeed the planet she had been longing to see.

In difficult situations, of which she had had quite a few, being the fearless kitten that she was, T'Beau liked to think of her grandma Dulcinea, who had always told her that politeness and kindness were the best and wisest route to take when dealing with people.

"Meep!" she therefore said politely to the big brown thing and right away she was rewarded with a reply: "*MOOO!*"

It gave T'Beau a big fright because it had been *very loud*.

"Oh," she thought. "Of course . . . I should have known that they would speak a different language here."

She tried again:

"Mee-ooh", she said, somewhat hesitantly but with increasing courage at the sight of the gentle eyes on the big brown thing.

"M-mmmm—oooooh!" it replied.

And then "Come along. I'll get you some milk. But afterwards we are going to have to work on your accent!"

LITTLE SWEETIE HAS A PLAN

It was a beautiful Sunday in late March. Jack, my partner at the time, and I were sitting outside under the redwoods basking in the warmth of the sun. We had an appointment later on to go view a car that was for sale on the other side of the bay, a little more than an hour's drive away, but for now, we were still relaxing and enjoying the day.

Little Sweetie, our big momma cat, came wandering over to us, meowing.

"Hey, Sweetie," said Jack, reaching out to pet her. "What's up, girl?"

Sweetie snuggled into his caress for a while. Then she meowed and kept walking. When she got to where I was, I ran my hands over her back. Two of the black spots there were so close to each other that when she sat in a certain way they always looked like a heart shape. It was too cute!

Little Sweetie as a kitten meeting Molly Labradoodle (Photo: Anonymous)

Sweetie was a beautiful kitty (all our cats were, of course!) with big inquisitive eyes. She was really smart and the undisputed matriarch, who had it all under control, always keeping a good eye on everything.

Right now, she was *'big as a cow'*.

"When are you going to give us your babies, Sweetie?" I asked, stroking her. "You look like you're ready to burst any moment!"

She arched her back and meowed again. Then she started walking down the trail towards the neighbors' but as soon as she got to the steps she turned around and came back up, meowing again.

She did that several times, until I said "Looks like Sweetie wants us to follow her . . ."

Jack laughed. "Haha," he said. "You mean as in 'Lassie'? Like, *'Come on, Timmy . . !'* ?"

I laughed as well. "Perhaps. She's a clever girl . . ."

"That's for sure," Jack agreed.

I kept watching Sweetie, who was still doing her loops.

"Let's just go and see what she wants."

"Alright then," Jack got up too, and together we followed Sweetie down the trail to the steps and past the first neighbor to the Harper's house.

At the time we lived about a half mile off Highway 9, not too close, but we always kept the traffic in mind. People often came from 'over the hill' in Silicon Valley, high on the adrenaline rush of their fast little super cars flying round the bends in the Santa Cruz Mountains, racing to get to the beach or other 'urgent' destinations. While we were aware that our cats went walking on down the drive we were also doing our best to make sure we didn't encourage them to get near the road.

Thankfully, the neighbor that Sweetie had wandered to was still quite a stretch from the highway.

Nevertheless we began to feel a little uncomfortable about her going there, and so eventually we said "That's far enough, Sweetie. Come on, we're going back up now . . . Let's go home!"

We started walking back up the bank to the house with Sweetie following us, reluctantly though, it seemed.

Once there, we sat down to continue our previous relaxing and enjoying while Sweetie decided to resume her meowing and pacing.

I'm sure it was less than half an hour later when I couldn't watch it any longer. I had to find out what she was trying to say. After all, we were both studying to be animal communicators, I thought. This was a pretty obvious opportunity for practice in my eyes.

"I think Sweetie still has something she wants to show us. I'm going to go down and see where she wants to take me." Then I turned to her and said, "Let's go, Sweetie. Show me what's up . . ."

I didn't have to tell her twice. She ran off down the hill again with me in pursuit. Down the bank and past the neighbor's we went. When we got the Harper's she disappeared under their house among garden chairs and other summer paraphernalia that were stowed there. There was a lattice that was big enough for a cat to get in but not for a human.

I stood and peered in. "I can't follow you in there, Sweetie . . ." I called. "It's too small for me . . . "

No problem for Sweetie. She walked all the way through to the other side and came back out there. Then, all of a sudden, she was gone.

I walked to the side of the house and looked up the banks there. No sign whatsoever of black and white 'football sized' Sweetie. Hm . . . She had to be around somewhere, she couldn't just vanish . . .

Well, actually, I do believe that cats can disappear and reappear at will, but I was sure this was not the case in this instance.

Walking up the side of the house a redwood stump caught my eye. Intuition began to beep with excitement.

I bet she's in there!

Feeling no desire whatsoever to stick my hand in a tree trunk I had not been properly introduced to I went back up to the house to fetch a mirror and a flashlight. When I shined it into the stump it confirmed exactly what I had expected: There was Little Sweetie, snug and cozy, curled up in her perfect hideaway. I could have sworn she was grinning at me.

I ran back to the house. "Jack!" I called breathless with excitemnent and from running up the hill. "Come on down! You gotta see this . . . "

"What is it . . . ?"

"Let me show you . . . !"

Jack groaned as he got up from his seat to follow me. "Where are we going?" he said.

"Wait for it, you won't believe what she's got, it's totally awesome . . ."

Down the trail to the steps, past the neighbor's we went, as before, then to the other side of the Harper's house while I gave my account of what had happened.

"She came all the way down here and then she disappeared. I figured she must be here somewhere, and guess what – " I pointed to the stump.

Jack looked amazed. "Are you saying – ?"

"Check it out!" I shined my light on to the mirror that I had pointed inside it.

There was Sweetie, looking cool as can be for him – and pretty darn smug for an expectant mother.

We were both full of praise. "Wow, Sweetie, what a lovely little 'cabin' you found yourself! Well done, pretty girl. You are awesome!"

Little Sweetie Sweetheart

Then we walked back up to the house, talking about what an amazing kitty she was to find that stump and lead us to it the way she did. It felt like we could be the next 'Flipper' or 'Lassie' people.

A little while later it was time for us to get into the car and drive over to Livermore to see the vehicle we were thinking of buying. It took almost three hours before we were back again.

As usual, all of our cats came running out to greet us as we drove up. All, except Sweetie, that is. We fed the hungry crowd and then called for her to come join us.

Sweetie didn't appear though. She's probably having a snooze somewhere, we said, and sat down to check emails and messages.

An hour later, when she still hadn't showed up, Jack and I looked at each other, saying almost in unison, "Let's go check that stump . . . "

Down the trail and the steps we went, past the neighbors' house and up the other side of the Harper's to the stump where we had seen her last.

I shined the light inside and said, "I think I can see her."

Jack reached in. He was braver than I was . . . then he smiled.

"What is it? What is it?" I got really excited.

He pulled out his arm and showed me what he held in his hand. It was a beautiful newly born kitten, black and white like Sweetie.

"The first thing I felt when I reached in . . ."

I let out a squeal of delight. "She's had her kittens, and all by herself! While we were gone . . !"

"How many are there?" I asked.

"At least three." Jack said.

We debated briefly if it was best to leave them where they were or if we should bring them all up to the house. The house won, and I ran up to get the kitten bed for safe and snug transport.

One by one Jack picked them out, handing them to me to put in the bed. There were five, all healthy and well. Sweetie came out last, accompanied by major praise from us. Then I took the bed and Jack followed me up to the house, carrying Sweetie. We had to stop halfway because she became anxious about her kittens until we showed her that I had them all, safe and sound in the basket bed I was cradling close to me.

We placed her in the closet where we knew the familiar smells and sounds would reassure her while at the same time give the kitties a perfect nursery.

Once all was taken care of we looked at each other and gradually it dawned on us what Sweetie's Master Plan had been all along.

"She knew we would be gone because we told her."

"She must also have known she would be having the babies this afternoon."

"And so she found the perfect place where she could have them all by herself *and* told us beforehand where she would be in case we came back and didn't find her . . !"

"She must have totally planned this. I wonder what she was thinking when we were so slow to get her meaning!"

I giggled, imagining Sweetie's comment: "Humans! I wonder if they ever use those big brains?"

KITTEN SCHOOL

Somewhere around mid-January there was a great big ruckus under the house and it became clear that Mr Grey, the neighborhood stray had gotten lucky. His wily ways had led him all the way to our pretty girls who were more than ready for him. I had not been living in the house for a fortnight yet when the kittens started dropping, roughly a week apart, until in the end the count stood at sixteen, and that didn't even include Jumper, who we later found out had secretly given birth in our neighbors' boat, dearie me!

Box of Sweets

Living in the mountains the way we did we were pretty safe from judgments because not many people knew about our kitten avalanche. We were well aware of the drive to have cats spayed in order to prevent too much procreation, but it is also important to know that at the time having a cat spayed cost over $200. That kind of money was not available in a house where someone was barely surviving by himself but had a good enough heart to take in cats in need.

We also knew that as soon as the birth was over our girls would be keen on finding Mr Grey again for some more hanky-panky.

That, of course we couldn't allow. Jack suggested we keep them in the house, but since that hadn't worked the first time round I was pretty much against it.

"They'll drive us insane!" I protested, setting brain cells and intuition to work.

On the side of the house below our bedroom window was a little garden that had a very nice wooden fence around it. I thought it would make a great kitty park. We secured the bottom areas with boards and got plastic net fencing to put on top in order to make sure our agile mommas wouldn't be able to climb over and escape to another dose of extra-marital pleasures. Then we put the long ladder under the bedroom window for outdoor access.

Every morning one of us would collect the kittens in a basket and hand them to the other who had come up the ladder to the bedroom window. Playtime for kitties! Then we would sit down to watch them run around us and play with their little friends and their mommas. Everyone was in heaven!

One morning we had it all set up like that again and were enjoying the happy scenes all around us when a movement at the top of the ladder caught our attention. It was Little Sweetie, mother, grandmother, auntie and general matriarch of our kitty clan. She had a little stuffed toy in her mouth, Pedro, the Highland cow, the only 'animal' I had been able to bring with me when I moved in.

The way she stood there looking down made it appear like she was saying: "And today, kittens, we will learn how to carry prey in our mouths. Attention now, class is starting!"

And then she proceeded down the ladder with Pedro in her mouth, rallying her tiny furry students around her.

Being able to watch Sweetie fulfill her teacher role with so much ease and grace felt like an enormous privilege. I had never seen outdoor kitten school quite like that. Both of us were fascinated and mesmerized by the experience.

PS I am quite aware of the predicament that shelters find themselves in, especially every spring time when kitten season comes around. There are so many little fur-babies that need homes, and I understand the need for spaying and neutering to prevent those places being completely flooded with new intakes.

Thanks to a foundation in Redwood City and the Santa Cruz County Animal Shelter that later offered low cost spaying we did eventually find a way for all our girls and boys to have the procedure.

And today we will learn how to carry prey in our mouth.

Sedona Spirit – The Real Skinny

Sandy threw her little roller case in the trunk of the car.

"That's my last bag loaded!" she called back to Greg. "How are you doing?"

"Just saying goodbye to Kitty Girl . . . I told her the neighbor will come and take care of them all." Then he yelled, "Buddy, come back here!"

"What's going on?" Sandy asked, walking over.

"Buddy caught a mouse." He chased away the misbehaving cat, managed to grab the traumatized mouse and quickly walked away from the house. Then he yelped. "Oww! That darn thing bit me!"

Sandy knew, even after this short time, that this was not the time for a joke so she bit her lip but couldn't stifle a tiny giggle.

She had been having glimpses of past lives, the two of them growing up among the red rocks in the desert, chasing each other on their horses, long hair flying in the wind. But even though she had mentioned that sense of 'blood brothers' a few times she wasn't sure if that meant anything to him or not. Heck, she didn't know what it meant to her, if anything!

"Where'd he bite you?" She asked as casually as possible.

"Right here, on my thumb. Ungrateful beast!"

Sandy nodded and stepped inside the house quickly. She could not control herself any more. I'm sorry, my potential blood brother, but it's just too funny that you are not seeing the humor in this . . .

Eventually everyone of the cats was taken care of and they headed off on their adventure.

"You know," he said as he pulled onto the highway. "I've had a vision last night about rescuing a kitten by the roadside. I wonder what that's all about . . ."

"That should be interesting," she replied, laughing. "Because obviously nine cats are not enough yet . . ."

Greg smiled. "Perhaps not . . . "

As the miles passed under their wheels they more or less forgot about the cat vision, though animals were always there, at least on the periphery. During breakfast at the Cameron Trading Post just past the Grand Canyon North rim they looked over a brochure from a cat sanctuary in Utah that Sandy had found. After discussing for a while the possibility of visiting to see how it was run and if that might be in their shared future too they opted instead to head east into Hopi territory. A grey fox they spotted from the distance seemed to approve the choice.

Their next stop was Kayante, where Greg wanted to see the Navajo Code Talkers exhibition, which meant they had to set foot in the local Burger King to admire it, a location that tickled Sandy no end.

When their heads were full enough of astounding pictures and stories they stepped back outside. The midday heat felt dense, wall-like. Three dogs were almost hugging the edge of the building trying hard to find cool relief in the narrow shade provided by the roof. They looked hungry and not well cared for, so they each got a few handfuls of dog food that Sandy and Greg had brought for that purpose. As they watched them wolf down the unexpected blessing they held out their hands to send them reiki as well until it was time to continue on to their next destination, Four Corners.

After the obligatory exercise of standing with both feet in the four states that came together at Four Corners, which was surprisingly rewarding, they wandered around the sales booths to take in the Native American arts and craftwork lined up all around the square. Sandy bought a medicine bag with beadwork that caught her eye. She wasn't sure whether she was tapping into a past life again or whether it was simply because of the movies she had seen growing up. It didn't seem to matter though, there was some other kind of energy there claiming her attention.

"Jack, do you think there might be a medicine man around here that we could talk to about . . . things . . .?"

"Let's find out!" he replied.

They got lucky at the third booth.

"Try Johnny Two Bags just down the road. He lives in a double wide just off the road to Farmington."

They listened to several detailed descriptions about how to find him and were assured that it would be perfectly alright to just show up and knock on his door.

Excited about what that new adventure would bring they headed off. The road was straight enough and the directions had sounded pretty simple.

After driving up and down several times trying to spot the double wide trailer with the medicine man their faces lost the excitement somewhat.

"Let's go a bit further down that way, perhaps we turned around too soon . . ." Sandy said.

Greg pulled in the next driveway and turned the car. "What was that?" he said then.

"What?"

"That box . . . did that say 'free kittens'?"

"I didn't see it. Is that what it said?"

"Pretty sure that's what it said . . . " He slowed down. "That's maybe what my vision was about . . . "

Ah . . . the vision . . . yes . . .

"Were there kittens in the box? Been a hot day . . ." Sandy was concerned.

"Not sure, I didn't see any . . ."

"You know," Sandy said, "I would say let's go have a look but you and I both know that we can't just go 'look at a kitten' because . . ."

" . . . we would take it . . ."

"Exactly . . . and what's more, because we could also not just take one, we'd have to take two because one would be lonely . . ."

"Hmm . . . I see what you're saying . . ."

"Still . . . it's your house and your cats . . . I'm only visiting . . ."

"Let's go see the box again . . ."

They drove slowly past the box and the sign that, sure enough, said 'FREE KITTENS'.

"I guess we can't . . ."

"No . . . I guess not . . ."

He turned around again but then slowed down once more.

Sandy smiled at him. "Your decision . . ." she said. "You'd have to keep it and take care of it.

"I know . . . but . . . what do you think . . .?"

"I'm thinking that if we shouldn't go and look at the kitties we'd be long gone and wouldn't be agonizing over it . . ."

"Alright!" He said and with one decisive move he turned the car back, heading for the box.

Right at the moment when they were ready to come off the highway a van pulled into the drive right in front of them. They followed on behind it along the dusty track for about a quarter mile because it seemed to know where it was going.

Eventually it stopped at a squat grey building. Dogs were running around and a girl came out of the house. She was young, early twenties perhaps, and looked like a Diné/Navajo native.

She was busy with the people in the van. Two big dogs came to check out Sandy and Greg. One of them apparently was a seasoned meditator. He sat very upright, gazing at Sandy, his eyes like gateways into the universe.

When the girl had finished with her visitors she walked over to them. Sandy shook herself out of the hypnotic interaction with the dog and stood up to meet her.

"We have come to see about your kittens," said Greg.

"Oh," she replied. "I have just given away my last two to the people before you. I only have this little one left here." She picked up a tiny little kitten and set it on Greg's hand where it almost disappeared, it was so small.

"Aw," he said. "This one is much too young to be taken away from her mommy . . ."

The girl thought for a moment, then decided to grab the opportunity. "I have a fourteen week old in the house that I could let go . . ."

Greg looked at Sandy. Then he nodded. "Let's see her!"

The girl went back inside. When she came out she had a little tortoiseshell kitten in her arms, which she handed to Greg. "Her name is Impostor . . ."

Greg took her carefully and walked away a couple of steps. Then he held her up to his face and asked, "Do you want to come to California with us? We have a nice cat family that you could join . . ."

He later swore that her reply was as follows: "What are we waiting for? Where's your car? PUT. ME. DOWN!"

That was pretty clear, so off they drove, Greg behind the wheel, Sandy in the passenger seat with 'Impostor' on her lap. It didn't take long for the little kitty to cuddle up.

There were no proper pet stores in the area, just a Walmart to get supplies. They bought cat food, a portable littler tray, a scoop and other cat paraphernalia. Not because their new friend had any idea what a cat toy was but because *they* couldn't resist. The next thing would be to get her a brand new name because she could not possibly remain 'Impostor.'

That night they sneaked the little kitty into the motel and shared their dinner with her. Apparently she liked that more than the cans they had got. Much more! Afterwards she curled up on the bed and purred for a long while before spending her first happy night nestled right between her new mom and dad.

The next morning after breakfast they cleaned up the room to make sure that cat visitors would not get a bad name. They had already decided to go back to Walmart for some cat and dog food for the ones still left at kitty's former home and a little cash to help the humans too.

Sedona: Hiking at Shiprock

"Did you see the way that dog looked at me?" Greg said afterwards. "That was like a meditation, and a long one at that!"

"Was it that dark one? Not sure what breed he is . ."

"No, he was tan, like a Golden mix or something."

"They're certainly some amazing animals she's got there . . ."

They puzzled about it for a little longer, then hit the road for Shiprock, another power place for Native Americans.

There was never any question about what to do with their new feline family member. It was perfectly clear from the start that she would just get on the hike with them. They only stayed for a couple of hours, but all the while the little kitty was following them. When she went off exploring she'd always came running back when they called her and even alerted them to animal presences they might have otherwise missed, like a little burrowing owl on the way down.

True to cat reputation their new kitty was as curious as anything. She spent the driving time wandering around the car, looking out this window and that, learning not to go into the foot wells, and from her quick uptake about the litter box they understood she was a highly intelligent girl.

The following day they were en route to Sedona. Heading down Oak Creek Canyon towards the town Sandy looked back to see what she was up to and laughed out loud. Kitty was sitting on the parcel shelf in the back of the car and appeared completely spooked. She was staring up into the sky with an extremely bewildered look on her face.

Eyes big and wild the size of saucers they could almost hear her say, "There are . . . *things* . . . sticking up into the sky where there should be *just . . . sky!*

Oh my . . . that little girl had grown up in a desert area and had never seen a tree before, only the dry shrubs around her birth place! She kept staring, eyes big and round. What on earth were they? That sure didn't look right . . . !

Sedona had a pretty crazy vibe that day and after things got too weird for them they decided to head out of town for a hike. Red Rock Crossing sounded like the perfect place, refreshing water surrounded by red rocks.

They wandered along the trail from the parking lot with the little tortie bouncing around, exploring. Soon they came to a tree trunk and heard a scraping noise "tch-tch-tch . . ."

Their kitty was expertly running her claws down both sides several times and before they knew it, she, who had only just seen her first real tree, shot up the trunk of a small oak like a rocket. In a flash she was up and before they could worry if she'd manage to get back down she was running alongside them again, tail high and visibly proud of her achievement.

There were more challenges to come though. When they got to Oak Creek they noticed she was getting nervous. What on earth was this stuff? *Water?* She had not seen running water before either . . . She kept staring at it, watching with cocked head the glistening reflections of the sky and the leaves in the constantly moving swirls of the creek.

Sandy and Greg wanted to get across to the bed of red rock in the center of the stream. It looked like the perfect place to rest for a while and take in Sedona magic.

"I don't think she's going to jump across," Sandy said, bending down to pick her up.

"Put me down, put me down, *PUT. ME. DOWN!*"

Again, the message was so clear she could almost hear her say it.

Sandy laughed. Thankfully it was only a narrow channel of water and she could let her go quickly.

They sat down and let the kitty explore some more. She appeared really happy on the huge rock bed but whenever she reached the edge and saw the water moving she got spooked again.

What an enchanting place this was. The massive pillars of Cathedral Rock were towering above them in all their sacred vortex majesty. They knew they wouldn't get any closer today but the view up was making enough of an impression for them to be satisfied with their little hike.

Sandy fully expected to carry their new kitty back across the various channels onto the trail but much to her surprise she saw her walk right to the edge, examine it again and then – take a good drink! This girl was a fast learner!

Sandy was speechless. Then she turned to tell Greg who said quietly, "I think we should call her Sedona . . ."

Sandy nodded. The name was perfect. Watching her move through her new world with the giant strides she had made deserved nothing less than a name as full of spirit as this one.

They were all tired as they got into the car and headed out of town, on the long road back to California.

After dinner, where Sedona got a hero's portion of catfish, they watched the full moon shining down as they were driving through the landscape. They kept stopping for the mystical sights in the desert, awed by unusual lights in the sky that kept following them all the way out of state.

The little kitty with the big spirit had curled up on Greg's lap, full of all her new experiences from this long, exciting day. Greg and Sally smiled at each other, happy for following their intuition about bringing her with them.

They thought that they understood what an amazing being Sedona was but it took them a good few months to realize that, against all appearances, they absolutely had *not* failed to meet the *medicine being*.

They just hadn't expected him to have four legs and talk in meows.

Stealthy Motel Kitty

Sapora Goes Wild

Butter would not melt in her mouth

Sapora had come to us as a foster kitty during my first year in the Santa Cruz Mountains. She was a black fluffy princess with a beautiful pink 'bling' collar, who had lived a sheltered life in a big house on a hill in Santa Cruz. In stark contrast to that, all our cats were indoor as well as outdoor cats and her previous people were a little doubtful about this.

"Do not let his cat out," they said. "She will never come back."

I had brought Sapora home on a stormy November night, where the rain was so bad you could barely see the hand before your eyes. Thankfully once I got back to the mountains the weather cleared up. We did our best to make her comfortable and gain her trust in order to help her integrate into our little family.

Like most cats I know, Sapora was an intelligent girl. Waking up in our cabin in the woods the next morning it didn't take her long to take her chances on the briefly opened door. One black flash and she was gone. I ran after her but – true to kitty nature - she didn't respond to my calls. She was on a mission!

I was freaking out. We had been told that she had been inside for a whole year and a half. There was no way she would have any mountain living skills like our kitties did. I was still worried sick when my partner at the time let Sweetie in and guess-who wandered in nonchalantly right behind her . . . ?

Well . . . Who said she wouldn't come back? Apparently that was not a problem!

Phew, that made things so much easier for all of us. If she'd go out and come back by herself we were all good.

It has to be said here that some cats seem to be perfectly happy being indoor cats, and letting them outside does bring certain risks. We live in an area where they may become dinner for predators and it is therefore important to take steps to keep them safe. I am of the firm opinion though that some cats would rather take the risk than never be allowed outside to see the sky again and run up their favorite trees. Sapora showed pretty clear signs which kind she really was in her soul, and I figured that that must have been why she had chosen us.

After her first little adventure Sapora walked over to the sofa, found herself a good spot and sat down to groom. All seemed well, but perhaps that extremely pleased look on her face should have made me take notice and her 'butter wouldn't melt in her mouth' demeanor should not have fooled me into thinking that she wasn't capable of playing the confidence trick game on me.

It was only a few hours or so later, around lunchtime, when I saw her standing by the door, and true to what I thought was our newly found understanding, I opened it to let her out.

When she hadn't showed up an hour later I knew that I had totally fallen for her trick, darn!

I walked around all over our little neighborhood searching, calling her name over and over again. Nightmare scenarios were running amok in my head, one 'what if' after another. How could she have disappeared so fast and so completely?

Many searches that afternoon and evening were without success. Eventually, just before midnight, I headed out one last time, against all odds, with not much hope of finding a black cat in the dark. Staggering around the uneven ground of the forest floor around our house, navigating roots and branches I kept calling 'Sapora! Sapora!"

I was just passing the redwoods outside the door where the path leads down the steps to the neighbor's when there was a 'black flash' and she suddenly appeared as if out of nothing right next to my feet.

"Sapora!" I yelled. "Where on earth have you been . . . ?"

I bent down to pick her up, cradling her in a steel grip. She was not getting out of this one!

"You're coming with me! No more running outside any more tonight."

She purred. What an adventure that had been! Her transformation from Black Fluffy Princess to Wild Mountain Kitty had kicked off to a promising start!

Of course I was not aware of her plan at the time. It dawned on me eventually that that was what she was up to, but it did cause me a few grey hairs until I finally got it. She came to us because she wanted, she *needed* to be able to go outside.

I almost heard her say it: "Well, what do you expect? If you had people, that you knew were hell-bent on keeping you locked up, would you voluntarily go back into their house? You give me freedom, I will come back. Deal?"

Yes, Sapora, deal. I could totally see her point. I would not want to live in a cage and it was not in my life plan to subject another being to that. The kitties that came to us chose us for that very reason. Cats who want to live indoors or in a catio will choose someone else for their people.

Sapora Knows a Secret

Sapora Mystic Kitty

It had been quite a peaceful evening in our little cabin in the Santa Cruz Mountains. All the cats were in good spirits and accounted for. Except for one, that is, our black fluffy Sapora who hadn't come in yet. I was just about to go look for her when I heard screeching and hissing outside. Running out the door in the direction of the noises I found her wrapped in a fight around Mr Gray, the neighborhood stray.

"Sapora, let go!" I yelled, stomping my foot to get their attention, and "And you - get out of here, Gray!"

That didn't have the desired effect, or rather, none at all. Neither of them listened to me and even though I did manage to break them up with another go, instead of finally getting rid of the aggressive visitor they both decided to run away.

I stayed out for a good while but no amount of calling made Sapora turn and come back to me. She was clearly not ready to come in just yet, so I gave up and headed back into the house.

It was quite a bit later at night by the time I realized that she still had not returned. Grabbing a flashlight and a jacket I walked outside.

"Sapora! Sapora!" I kept calling and listening for a sound from her. She would often hide out in the banks just past our neighbor's house from where she would answer me with her special sweet little *m'ow*.

Shining my light around the area for her dark fluffy outline I walked past the house and our little garden to the corner where the neighbor's property line was. The ground there sloped down to a small nearby road and I had often seen our other cats come up it on their way home. I was hoping I would get lucky again here tonight.

It looked like I might be because finally, my light was reflected by two cats' eyes.

"There you are!" I called, relieved. "Sapora! Come here! Here, kitty kitty!"

When she didn't come running as she would usually have done, I tried again. "Come on, kitty kitty! Sapora! Come here . . .!"

Something felt a little odd though . . . Weren't Sapora's eyes much more greenish than this? These were more orangey . . . it just didn't look quite right.

I stood watching as the animal slowly moved up the bank, its eyes still reflecting in my light. They kept getting higher and higher off the ground making it more doubtful by the second that I might be looking at my little cuddly girl.

This was an unusual cat somehow. It had stopped now and was slowly nodding its head from left to right and back again. Sniffing perhaps . . .? What strange fascinating movements though . . .

That was definitely not an ordinary cat I was looking at. In fact, this was not a house cat at all. I was staring at a mountain lion.

I just stood there, unable to move, watching the scene in front of my eyes, completely mesmerized. The idea of getting away and into the house didn't even occur to me.

Unable to move, still shining my flashlight, I watched as he walked up to the fence in perfectly smooth big cat style, about fifteen feet away from me, looked and then turned right, heading up the bank, tail straight up in the air.

A minute or two later I saw the motion activated light at the neighbors' in the street above us come on, which finally broke the spell I had been under.

Ah, I thought. So that's where you are now!

At no point in time did I ever feel the need to run to safety, even though the puma could have easily jumped the four foot fence between our neighbors and us. I suppose he wasn't really interested to investigate what must have appeared as a light source without any nutritional value whatsoever.

Grabbing hold of my senses again I looked around some more for Sapora, but without much conviction that I would manage to find her. I was pretty sure she knew better than to show herself that night. In fact, I didn't see her again until well into the next morning, at bright daylight, when true to her style she came sauntering in as if nothing out of the ordinary had happened at all during the night.

The Fabulous Miss Mizzle

Saturday night cat sitting, just after Christmas. I'm downstairs on the sofa, doing stuff on my iPad, only barely watching TV.

Hikaru, the orange 'shrimp kitty' has been snuggling next to me for the last hour or two. I can never quite figure out if he loves me or the hand crocheted blankie more. The blanket zaps him with static electricity but my good old-fashioned belly rubs are a serious contender. It's a close race, I think.

Mizzle: Where's your bike?

Next thing I know there's a "Meow, meow, MEOW" coming from the stairs.

I turn around. It's the upstairs tiger kitty enticing me to follow her.

"Mizzle . . . !" I say. "What's up . . . ?"

"Meow, meow, meow! MEOW!"

"Are you kidding? It's not bed time yet. Way too early for me . . ."

But she's not giving up. "Meow, meow, meow, meow . . . !"

Looking back at the TV, I have to admit she's got a point. It's been really lame, and not just tonight. There's nothing I could do here that I couldn't also do in bed.

"Okay then," I say. "But I'm still going to watch stuff!"

I grab my things, tell Hikaru to come join us once he's done zapping himself and get moving.

Mizzle runs up ahead of me. She's not called me to bed before, that's definitely a first. I'm curious to see what she's got on her mind . . .

Upstairs Mizzle squints as I turn on the lights.

"What . . . ?" I laugh. "You know well that humans are not lucky enough to have eyes like yours that can see in the dark . . ."

Next I give the wood stove a nod. I call it Marvin . . . the white round shape reminds me of the robot from the Hitchhikers Guide movie. I feel a bit sorry for him because the design works much better on a wood stove. (No offense to Douglas Adams, it's the movie design people that failed to grasp the chance of a lifetime. Marvin, the 'paranoid android', should have been awesome.)

I put my iPad down, informing Mizzle that I'm not ready yet: humans have all kinds of stuff to do before they're allowed to go to bed.

Finally it's all taken care of. I carefully lift the covers and get in next to Mizzle, the night lover kitty, who usually pretends not to know me during daylight hours. Reaching out to pet her, she rewards me with a sweet throaty purr.

Ahhh . . . that sound never fails! A world with a purr is a good world . . .

I grab my iPad from the side table and open it up.

"So . . . Mizzie . . . what shall we watch . . . ?"

This could take a while. Netflix has been awful recently, loads of crap movies, violent to the extent of being gory or full of dystopia and worse, topping it off with male leads that apparently have never come across razors and their stunning capabilities of making people look nice.

But, tonight apparently, we're in luck. 'The Art of the Steal' looks like it could be a hoot. Click to load and off we go . . .

The beginning credits are already fun. Mizzle has her head on my arm and I notice, much to my surprise, that she must be watching the movie. Her eyes are getting big with fascination, rolling left, right and up and down with the movement in front of her, following the names on the screen as they are flying in and out in all directions.

Once the scene is set and the plot is moving along Kurt Russell shows us how to ride a motorbike like a boss. Fast. Furious! We watch, captivated. Man, what a chase, this really is fun . . . Mizzle's eyes are getting bigger and bigger, I can almost hear her go 'vroom vroom!' with her head hooked on the bike chase. She looks

The Kitty-Human Pact

like she has half a mind to jump on the back seat. In her excitement she starts pawing the screen . . . I'm not really sure if she wants to catch the riders and eat them or just turn up the speed some more.

Race over, we all take a breath. Kurt Russell is safe for now, phew. We can get back to more gentle plot moving. But apparently paintings and art heists are not as much up Mizzle's street as fast chases. I can tell she's losing interest. Hm . . . what to do . . .

A thought comes to mind. A number of years back I tried to get my cat's attention, which led me to the weird and wonderful world of movies made for felines. Pulling up YouTube, I do a search on 'videos for cats'.

Voilà, what a selection . . . videos with birds, fish and all kinds of other attractions.

Hikaru: Manifesting Shrimp

"Wanna watch some birdies, Mizzle?"

She stares at me in the half dark. I'm not entirely sure if she has a scathing look on her face, perhaps sending me a thought along the lines of 'what is it with humans and baby language . . . ?'

I decide to ignore it though and click on the first option.

It's a real video of birds . . . okay . . . They flutter around, chirping and singing . . . hm . . .

"They're pretty, aren't they?" I say, looking over at her.

She pretends not to be interested at first, but then the movement and tweeting grabs her. Guess who's getting excited?

Suddenly her paw shoots across my screen so fast I can hardly follow.

Tap! Tap! And another one, *tap!*

Now she's totally getting into it and I'm beginning to fear for my iPad. Cat claws and screens? Not sure if that spells danger or damage . . . Perhaps I should err on the safe side and put on something less exciting.

Two quick clicks. "Here," I say. "How about these fish . . . ?"

Pretty goldfish swimming from left to right . . . right to left.

Tap . . . tap . . . much slower, less scratching . . . waaaay better!

I'm breathing a sigh of relief. Looks like my screen, like Kurt Russell, is out of danger.

Mizzle gives me a 'look', stretches, then yawns.

I can swear she's making that 'you're getting old and boring' face.

Never mind. It's time to turn off the iPad and the light.

"Goodnight, Mizzie . . ." I say as I lie down.

Prime Focus

She scrambles up into the crook of my elbow and purrs.

Ahhh . . . all is forgiven . . . purr . . . purr . . .

"Admit it, Mizzie, that was fun!"

"Purr . . . PURR . . . snore . . ." she says, her legs kicking a little bit, perhaps to get the bike started, as she's riding off into dreams that mere humans know nothing about.

The Full Mizzle Mystery
Photo: Brenda Laurel

Closing my eyes I drift into dreamland too, wondering if that was Kurt Russell there, on the back seat with her.

Kitty Dreaming: Forrest and Sierra

Forrest and Sierra usually come running when I arrive because they know it's food and cuddles time, which is always welcome. But this time I was surprised to find that only Sierra showed herself. I petted her hello and we walked into the house together where she got her long-awaited food – she was starving, of course! – fresh water and lots of love.

After I had got everything done for her I checked the house to see if Forrest was napping somewhere and had not realized that goodies were on offer. I went through every room, calling his name, and when that didn't yield a black fluffy boy I went outside to do the same there.

Sierra: One perfect kitty!

It was later in the morning by now and getting pretty hot already, so I figured he might be snoozing in a quiet place somewhere but again, no luck. But Forrest was a smart kitty, one that spent a lot of his time outside and I just had to trust that he was not going to do anything foolish that would put himself in undue danger.

For now I had to leave though I decided to work my day in such a way that I could add another visit in the evening.

It was around six thirty when I arrived back that day. Again, Sierra came running up to me but no black fluff-boy anywhere.

After feeding and cuddling Sierra I started walking around the grounds calling Forrest. Sierra joined me and we did several rounds of trying to find him, looking in awkward places to make sure he wasn't trapped or lying injured somewhere and listening closely for any replying meows. Nothing.

At this stage I still wasn't too worried yet because the bowl I had left on the counter for him as per my instructions had been empty, which gave me hope that I had simply missed him. Nevertheless I contacted his people and was told he may also have wandered over to the neighbors for more company.

I was already driving off when something black showed up in the corner of my eyes. It was dusk by then and I couldn't really say for sure. Pulling back in to park and running up to the house again in the hope that my eyes hadn't tricked me I had to admit defeat. He wasn't there, and he hadn't run inside either. What I had seen were probably the black plant pots in the garden, who may have appeared to be moving in my mirror as I was driving off.

That night I had a very strange dream. I saw a fluffy black cat that had strips of fur missing and was really thin. My heart sank in my sleep at the sight. But I looked again and again, I could not see any blood or injuries, so perhaps I was not being shown a dead animal that had been someone's dinner. I wondered if it was my own kitty Sapora, who was no longer with me or that of my friends' who had a similarly black long-haired boy. Was it Donald telling me he was about to leave us? Another of their cats had had procedures that required shaving fur off, perhaps I was processing that?

Whatever it was, I woke up more than a little disturbed and worried. I made sure to get myself up to the house as soon as I could manage.

As before, Sierra came running out for food and cuddles but no Forrest. Text exchanges with their mommy yielded the tip that he might respond to vigorous shaking of the treat container. Much to my relief they paid off, resulting in the appearance of a disheveled wild black thing that was quickly identified as the missing culprit. Geez Forrest, look at you! The masses of burrs and stickers as well as the dust on him made it quite clear that 'someone' had had a great time romping outdoors!

I was extremely relieved to see him, rewarding his reappearance with a fine number of treats for both of them, receiving little nose kisses in return as they got busy munching.

Forrest was apparently really pleased with himself. Going out on the 'ran dan' and then coming home to treats and cuddles must simply be the best of all worlds - except perhaps for his people being away.

After all the treats had been polished off he licked his chops and literally fell over to roll on the ground. Was it an invitation for tummy rubs? I figured it was and didn't hesitate to comply. But my, what did I find . . .! Not only was he covered in all kinds of 'fruits of the forest', he was also completely matted underneath. You're not a fan of doing that grooming thing, are you, Forrest . . .?

Thankfully this was a household with great tools. Apparently he didn't mind me going inside for brushing and grooming items and waited patiently for his personal slave to reappear in happy anticipation of some serious spa time.

Forrest's patient nature made it a relatively easy task. He only complained a few times very quietly when I got too close to the skin for me to prevent pulling. As I was working my way around his tummy and his side I suddenly noticed that there was a lot less fur in certain places, probably where mats had been removed previously by his mommy. It looked pretty much like my dream, not quite as clean shaved but close enough, I figured. I was relieved to find such an easy, gentle explanation to my dream that had worried me quite a bit.

For the time being though, we had used up all of Forrest's patience for lying still and being fussed with. He was a sweet and forgiving boy who allowed me to get a good section of his tummy done but now his 'wild kitty' had taken over and he had to run away to tend to other business.

Go, Forrest!

Forrest: Spa session takes it out of you

JESSIE AND SAPORA: THICK AS THIEVES

For cat aficionados like me it is a matter of course that any cat that appears to require help is given it immediately without concerns for the sacrifices it may require. That's all very well when you can reason it out with your spouse or whoever may be living in your house but is a very different story with other feline residents.

A little while before I had moved in my then partner had adopted a black cat who lived a lonely existence in his friend's garage. Jesse had lost her only buddy, a tuxedo named Sylvester, to a car accident and had become a sad and isolated girl. When Jack showed up for a visit she spotted her chance and, coming down from the rafters she climbed right into his lap, leaving him no real choice but to embrace her into his fold. And, to be fair, she didn't have to twist his arm much.

Sapora came to join us a few months after my introduction into the household. This sweet fluffy princess had drawn the short straw when her family moved to another place and declared they could only take their dog. My heart broke hearing the story and, listening beyond the words, I let myself be taken in by the thoughts that it was only temporary until we could find a nice suitable home for her.

At that time there must have been around five or six cats in the little cabin. Just after I arrived we had the kitten avalanche and even though we found good homes for most of them, some of them were allowed to stay with us. As they outgrew the kitten-charms and started to claim their places in the household things began to get a little tricky. Having already had prime position due to kitten cuteness and antics, some of them were indeed a little spoiled. Nevertheless it all seemed to work reasonably well. Or so we thought . . .

After a while we noticed that Jesse was showing signs of issues. First she got dermatitis and try as we might, we couldn't seem to get to the bottom of it. Then she stopped using the litter boxes, presenting us with puddles and finally poopy gifts on the bed. She also became very vocal. We were tearing out our hair trying to help her feel better. It was pretty clear to me that getting upset was only going to make things worse. Even the vet was at a loss.

At some point we came up with the last possible explanation, that Jesse suffered from overcrowding and that she might do much better as a single kitty where she didn't have to share space or attention with other feline competitors. After much discussion we decided to keep our eyes and ears open and if it looked like that was what she really wanted we would find her ideal place.

But first we got a response from a family who were interested in taking Sapora and made an appointment for them to visit and see how they would take to each other.

The day came and all morning we kept telling Sapora to let us know clearly if she wanted to go with them or not. If she didn't like the people she was welcome to stay until we found someone she resonated with.

Just after 2pm a car drove up and out came two, three, no, five ladies, mother and four daughters. All were excited to meet their potential new kitty.

We welcomed them into the tiny cabin and offered the younger girls a seat on the sofa while I took mom and eldest daughter into my room to meet Sapora. We had kept her inside all morning to make sure she didn't do a runner on us without meeting the possible new family.

Both mother and daughter thought she was exceedingly pretty and petted her happily, but no matter how hard I tried to get

Sapora to engage with them it felt a little strained. She kept act-ing a bit snooty and detached.

I was confused. She didn't act like she hated them them . . . What was going on there? I couldn't figure it out.

Eventually we decided to leave her to it and came back out to re-join the others in the living room.

The scene that met us there was interesting. Jesse, who looked like a veritable punk with her hair all spiky from the coconut oil we had applied that morning to ease her sores had come down from her cardboard ivory tower and as sweetly as proudly taken up residence right in between the girls. Apparently she had been going from lap to lap charming the socks off the younger girls while I had been trying hard in the next room to get Sapora to warm up to our guests.

Jack just shrugged. Of course he knew Jesse's tricks, he'd fallen for them himself a couple of years earlier und was fully aware

Jesse: ACTION!

that she was not to be underestimated. Nevertheless we were both stunned as the ladies declared unanimously that even with full disclosure of her issues Jesse Punk was their choice and they didn't need a fine princess after all, despite the fact that Sapora had turned into a fully qualified Wild Mountain Kitty.

What could we say . . . ? We packed up Jesse's belongings, which was done soon enough, added a towel and a cushion to help her with the transition and waved the lot good-bye as they drive down the hill towards Highway 9.

After they had left we looked at each other.

"What just happened?" I asked, bewildered.

"Beats me . . . " he replied.

"Did they really choose Jesse over Sapora?"

"Apparently so . . ."

"Geez . . ." We were both speechless.

It took us the rest of the day before it finally sank in. Some time after dinner, sitting out on the porch we eventually pieced it together.

Jesse and Sapora had been in on the whole thing together. It was the only explanation.

We tried to figure out how they had planned it.

"Okay, " Jesse must have said. "You go and play the cool princess while I go around and do 'my thing.' Just make sure they don't come out too soon. I'll need a little bit of time before I can be sure I got it down for good."

"You got it," would have been Sapora's reply. "I'll hold them off for a while pretending that I'll come round . . . in just a few more minutes." She might have added with her typical sly smirk, "I can keep that going forever . . ."

COVERED IN CATS

Donald lived in a household with four other cats and two large black dogs. He was a medium long-haired beauty with plenty of self-confidence that also allowed for mega charm and sweetness. Like many cats I have come to know and love his spirit was much bigger than his body, which was probably the reason why he often acted like he actually was the third black dog.

Donald: Everything under control!

I am pretty sure I met him before the night the Bear Fire started but that particular time was the occasion when we really bonded. His mom had received evacuation orders in the early hours and I had gone up to help her out by taking the cats and dogs to my place, which was just a long enough distance down the road for us to feel better about their safety.

Donald didn't know me very well at the time and when I cradled him to me in order to help him into the carrier as we had done with the others the stress of the situation got the better of him and he peed all over me. Poor baby, he felt the fearfulness of this unusual situation and had no other response available. I held him tight for a moment longer to help reassure him he was safe before we loaded everyone into my car.

Thankfully enough, even though firefighters and air drops would be struggling for weeks to control the fire until it was finally put out, evacuation orders were lifted for that area later that morning so that kitties and dogs could go back to their familiar homes again. By then Donald had established himself firmly in my heart.

During my house and pet sitting periods at his home he was always the highlight with his soft fluffy sweetness and gentle meow. At night, once all the work was done, he would immediately join me, at first choosing my lap but eventually settling in right under my chin, draped across me like a fine mink stole, leaving just enough vision so that I could watch a little movie or something to relax after a long day.

His affection saved my sanity many times when I felt too exhausted to get up for more than bed at the end of the night, while his choice of cuddling station left enough space for the others to join in. I'd often have Tommy in my lap, sometimes Buckaroo on my legs and Blondie with her cute goaty 'meh' rubbing her head on mine to my left. I guess it's a good thing that horses generally don't care for sofas because with the addition of two or three large dogs on either side we were pretty much full house.

Those were always my favorite times. Cats can be capricious and oftentimes they really do know how to get you to run around after them but beyond the silky furs and adorable paws there is such an inexplicable sweetness and mystery that just surpasses all the hassle by miles and miles, making it all worthwhile.

It must have been after one of those house sitting experiences during a solstice celebration with friends that I suddenly realized I wanted to choose a native name. I had no idea what it was but I knew one thing for sure: its meaning would be *Covered-in-Cats*.

Shortly after that solstice there was a period when Donald kept showing up in my dreams. One was particularly memorable. I was standing high up in an ancient building, like a castle ruin, looking down a steep cliff to a body of water below. While I was still admiring how steep and treacherous the rocky mountainside was, Donald shot past me, out from the opening in the wall where I was standing, flying down to the water like a squirrel from a tree, his black fur streaming in the wind.

I stood there, stunned, feverishly trying to figure out what to do. I had seen enough of the cliff to know that it would take me hours to make it down there, if I managed at all, unfit as I was.

While I was still wracking my brain to come to the right decision he suddenly appeared back at my side with barely a little

more than a casual 'Hi, how are you.' No big deal, right?

My relief was instant, accompanied by a huge sigh. But the question of what the dream was trying to tell me has been lingering for a good while. I'm guessing the exploration of its message would be quite another story. Whatever it may be, my hunch is that cats will keep surprising me for a very long time.

My first pledge as 'Covered-in-Cats' is to *absolutely* let them!

Feline Secret Service: Jack & Matahari

When I went to meet Jack and Matahari it looked like they were perfectly alright with me. I was therefore a little surprised to find that they didn't want to come out from under the bed for the first few visits that I was on my own with them. Thankfully enough I had asked about their favorite hiding places, otherwise I might have had to worry that they had done a runner . . .

Jack: Keeping an eye on it all

I could tell their presence from the fact that the food was gone and the litter boxes had been used when I arrived for my mornings or afternoons. All of that was encouraging but I nevertheless felt the need to make sure they were doing well in other ways too. While I was soon having increasingly more success luring Jack out from behind the bed with my feathered pole-dancing peacock toy, Matahari was a different kettle of fish altogether. For her, more drastic action was called for.

Their 'safe room hidey hole' was under the bed in the guest room behind two storage drawers. It proved pretty much impossible to draw Matahari out from under there. After a while it dawned on me that neither of them really had much of a clue about how important I was. Now that was something that clearly needed to change!

I lifted the mattress, which was surprisingly heavy, and sat down on the slats propping it up on my shoulders (I was really glad no one saw me leave that day with my bed head. The neighborhood might have started talking) . . . Then I reached out to Jack who let me pet him right away and after some further efforts Matahari let me stroke her head too. A very promising development, I thought, leaving full of confidence that day.

When I returned the next morning however, everything was back to square one - me, the big scary stranger and the kitties who stuck together against the enemy invasion. It was almost as if I had not completed my vetting process successfully just yet! We went through the same rigmarole as the day before but whatever progress we made with each other was again forgotten next time I returned.

Okay, kitties, y'all are missing out big time! Have you not heard of the first class cuddles that you could be enjoying? I am famous for my back scratches and tummy rubs!

But there is no being on the planet as stubborn as a cat . . . They just won't listen! (Or perhaps my security clearance was late coming through, who knows . . . ?)

When I arrived the following day I walked up to the front door as usual, and as I was unlocking the door I happened to look through the window into the kitchen, just in time to see a black and white fluff ball make a dash for the safe zone under the bed. "She's here, Matahari! Quick, hide!"

Were they having parties when I wasn't around? Or worse perhaps, dangerous encounters with double agents . . ? The scratch tree had been toppled over on more than one occasion and I shuddered to think what they were doing to the kitty grass as soon as my back was turned.

It was clear that I had to make some more changes. Despite initial hesitation I decided to pull out one of the two drawers that were making up the kitty fort. Then I got the food bowls and set them on paper towels in front of the bed, just a little underneath, so they wouldn't be too exposed but instead had a feeling of safety in the half darkness.

All the while I could tell that my every move was being followed by curious yet cautious eyes hiding under the bed.

"Yes, you two . . . Watch closely now. These are dinner bowls in my hands. See who is putting out the food for you . . . ? You probably thought it just appeared by magic? Far from it! It's ME that's filling them and you might just want to keep on my good side, if only for the sake of your meals! Now . . . What on earth is going on here? There's nom-noms for the ones that talk . . . "

Matahari: I'm watching YOU!

"Really . . ? You think you can buy us with some - ooooh, are those . . . *treats* . . . ?"

"They are indeed . . . Would you like to try some . . . ? I hear they're really tasty . . . and all it takes is some cooperation, isn't that a good deal!"

I picked up some of their kibble and let it clank into the bowl with four eyes from way back in the darkness firmly on me. Ahhh, did I see a tiny twitch there . . . ?

They were trying hard to hide it behind their poker faces but ever so small indications of movement betrayed that I had got their interest and attention now. It looked like I might finally be getting results . . .

What broke the resistance in the end was a trail of kibble from the bowls a little ways towards the back of the bed where they were crouching. The food in front of their faces proved way too tempting not to abandon their suspicious act. Slowly they edged forward and started munching. Much to my surprise Matahari didn't flinch once when I reached out to pet her.

"See . . . That wasn't so hard! Why don't you let me scratch your cheek a little bit . . ."

"Well, if you absolutely have to . . . But don't think for one second that I'm going to . . . purrrr-purr-purrrrr-purrrr. Ooops . . ."

"Ah, you are really a very lovely kitty, Matahari, once you let go of the shyness and suspicion, right? And you Jack, would you like to get some cuddles too?"

"Yea . . . Nahhh, actually, I'm cool. I'm going to go chase some 'things' now. Unless you have any more of that crunchy stuff . . ?"

A few days later, in the afternoon as I was leaving I noticed a kitty in the window when I looked back at the house. There was Jack, looking gorgeous as always with his black and white mane, catching flies or spiders apparently, and having a very entertaining time of it. He was quite the hunter despite having only one eye. But it was not just the chase that was keeping him busy. When I got into the car to drive off he interrupted his busy schedule and sat watching me, looking like a precious framed painting behind the window pane that reflected the Redwood trees by the house.

From then on we were playing 'milestones' . . . Jack had won 'First out from under the bed' and 'First to play with me' but now apparently it was Matahari's turn to surprise me. Having been majorly more skittish from the beginning she won 'First purr' and 'First kitty in my lap', while Jack still spent more time playing and chasing as he had done from the beginning. I guess the hunt was more his domain.

Matahari also was the first one to start conversations with her sweet melodic voice. "Meooow. . . Meow . . . ?" Meaning, Can I go play with your shoes?

She was a classy kitty. So polite too.

I nodded. "Feel free . . ."

I was incredibly pleased with my success and not a little proud. But I also couldn't help myself: "Ah, Mata Hari . . . " I said. *"Didn't I tell you, I haf vays of making you tok . . . "*

She paused, squinting at me from behind the coffee table, sizing me up again.

"Just because I accept you doesn't mean I'm going to stop watching you."

Ah. I see. . . Once a spy always a spy, I guess.

Simba, The Lion Cat King

Simba means lion in Swahili. Thanks to the educational nature of our modern culture that sweeps though all but the remotest corners of the world, most of us know that from a movie called The Lion King.

A stately Maine Coon that weighed in at 17lbs, Simba definitely had lionesque traits. But his regal appearance also

Simba: A Very Royal Feline

hid a very sweet gentle nature. I would have never expected him to be as dainty as he was taking treats from my hands without so much as a little nibble on my fingers. It made for a great game that we both enjoyed very much.

He did like toes though, apparently found them downright irresistible. But he paced himself there too. I was grateful that I was never in danger of losing any when we were cuddling on the sofa, or at night when my feet were sticking out from under the covers looking for some cool air. Even his early hour paw check of my head and face was not overly disturbing and he was too much of a gentleman to insist that I wake up to attend to whatever it was that made him do it. For all I know he might have been doing research on human intelligence and didn't want my ego interfering with his findings. Because for all their cute furry softness, we don't *really* know what cats are about or what they're after, do we . . .

From the beginning Simba and I connected like old friends. Could it really be that easy? Apparently so . . . After having met him twice just briefly I moved into the house for the duration of his people's trip East. We learned each other's routines and were careful to harmonize them so that we both could enjoy our week of living together with the least disruption. Going about it with the respect and polite consideration of an old married couple we soon became professionals at it.

"Interesting, what you are doing
there . . ."

There was one thing though that marred our old-new bliss a bit: I could not allow him the freedom to join me outside. It was our Indian summer, late October, and the sun was blasting down. The light and heat was something I really wanted to take advantage of but oftentimes I felt guilty walking out the door having made sure he stayed inside. It was for his safety, true, and for the peace of mind of his people but I really felt for him.

When I was sitting by the table outside the front door reading or attending to other things hearing his unique meowing that always sounded a little hoarse tugged at my heart. I usually didn't last too long once he started. How could I sit there peacefully with him inside, sometimes longingly looking out from behind the screen . . ? It just couldn't be done!

The only thing that kept me from getting completely heartbroken was the fact that his mommy had mentioned some ideas she had been considering of how he could be let out and still be safe. For now, I had to be firm though.

Apart from that, being a cat in a bright, beautiful, generously sized and well laid out house was perfect for Simba. He kept himself busy doing all the mandatory cat things like ignoring both of his fancy cat trees for the sake of a duffelbag in the master bedroom or a beautiful fleece by the window in the guest bedroom. Of course there were also times when he suddenly started tearing through the house at breakneck speed for no apparent reason. Other instances he tucked himself away quietly until I'd hear a faint meow that required investigation.

At first his meowing was a bit unsettling because I wasn't familiar with his voices. Was he proudly announcing success and achievement using the litter box or did he rather sound like he was complaining about issues doing his 'business'? I knew he was due a vet visit, so that would be looked into to make sure everything was in order.

One night I was watching a movie when all of a sudden I heard Simba's meow calling me away. Following the sound I carefully went down the stairs to see if he was having problems. He was in the room where his box was, sure enough, but nowhere near it. Instead I saw him over by the patio door, cowering down with big eyes and flailing tail, all excited.

Then I noticed a small speck move in the half darkened room. He was chasing a spider. His meow had been the hunting call announcing that he was about to make his big move and win against a dangerous and highly unpredictable opponent. His very demeanor made it quite clear that his victory would be glorious and worthy of an entry into The Annals of Simba The Great, Of the House of H—. And of course he would also be saving my life in the process, that went without saying! I could tell it was really important to him so I left him to it and went back upstairs.

Speaking of, I am not entirely sure if one night he tried to convince me of his connection with the 'Scottish Stewart' kings. When I pointed out to him that that was only his address and it was actually spelled 'Stuart' he became a little quiet and neither of us pursued the subject any further. I did however go to great lengths to make sure that he knew I was well aware of his royalty.

Can't go around denying nobility to the Lion Cat King now, can you . . .

Silver Hires A Body Guard

Like Sapora, Silver had come into my life as a foster kitty. His mommy had died and a cold-hearted relative had threatened to abandon him out in the woods to fend for himself. When my friend sent me his pictures knowing that there was no way I could resist his haunting eyes and fascinating personality I just had to take him in. Of course!

Who could resist those eyes?

He was unique, like all cats, and I'm fully aware of the contradiction there. Stubborn as any I had ever met he made his way to my bed on the very first night (come to think of how easy that was for him I suddenly understand why many men can't stand women who like cats!).

His voice was pretty amazing, demands for attention and food were usually loud, but he was also happy to just find a place to sit near me – or on top, as the case may be.

Silver and I had some wonderful times together but after a little over a year together my circumstances changed and I was 'told' *"New home. Silver. NOW."*

Such a good boy in the Basket

I had tried before to find him the perfect place but never succeeded and simply handing him over to a rescue as some people suggested would not have felt the right thing to do. This time, however, very quickly a wonderful lady, Patricia, showed up with her daughter Anna. They fell in love with him, and I was happy that they were willing to give him a new loving home where he still had the freedom to go out roaming or sit on the back deck all day long watching birds to his heart's content.

For me the best part was that I was still able to spend time with him on the occasions that I was asked to cat sit. He'd sleep with me in the master bedroom and in the morning after breakfast we would sit outside together, admiring the birds and trees.

I was often out during the day but after dinner in the evenings we would cuddle up on the sofa, or he'd sit on the pirate's chest coffee table to watch me. I was never quite sure what he was expecting to see when he did that, but who knows, perhaps he was learning to read auras the way Bubu did?

Cats are highly intelligent beings and Silver had me sussed pretty quickly, just like the rest of them. I love my freedom and to me that meant that I would respect an animal's desire for it as well. Of course there is a fine balance required because we also need to do our best to keep them safe.

When Silver 'tried it on with me' after dark (meow-meow-*MEOW!* to persuade me to allow him a night hunting adventure, which I was totally unable to agree to at all) he very quickly realized the way to get around the issue of his safety: He needed a bodyguard and – I was *IT!*

I am still not quite sure how he managed it but somehow he established a tradition of taking me out on a walk late at night. We'd go out by the front door, me armed with a 'million lux flashlight' to scare off anything untoward and then we'd wander around the neighborhood for a little while. He could sniff and check things to his heart's delight or use the outdoors litter box while I was doing my secret service impression, carefully scanning our environment for hidden threats while looking inconspicuous and really important at the same time . Once we had made sure that everything was safe and secure we could go home and relax in the good conscience of a job well done.

Does he really need a bodyguard?

I'm pretty sure Silver knew all about not fraternizing with the staff but how could I say no when nothing beats a sweet kitty cuddle at night, right? That is . . . if he didn't get me to do a second round outside in the dark of night . . .

THE THESPIANS – JASMINE AND MERCURY

Jasmine came to me as a victim of the insanely expensive and restrictive housing situation in California. After having received a 60 days notice for their rental home her mom and three kids had found themselves unable to secure a new place that would accept their cats. The only solution we could come up with was for me to take Jazzy on as a foster while a friend gave their second kitty a home.

She was a solid gray cat, but a little fluffier than Pebbles had been, and like the others, very pretty. It must have been a tough transition for her from a bustling family home to my quiet place. But even though my birthday buddy and neighbor Billie came to visit to help her settle down and feel comfortable I could not shake the feeling that she wasn't accepting the situation completely.

When the Bear Fire happened and my house turned into kitty evacuation station for seven displaced fur-balls Jazzy was not in favor of sharing her new home, however tentatively she might have been occupying it. She made her displeasure so crystal clear that I was furiously going through options of what might help them all de-stress and bring peace back into the house.

My neighbors Nickie and John had already agreed to our use of their downstairs guest space for the three dogs that were part of the evacuation posse, so that was out. However, we had been throwing around the idea of them taking in Jasmine after they had lost their own kitty only a short while before through a car accident. At the time their feelings had been that it was too soon after their loss, which was where we had left it.

Funnily enough Jazzy had quickly displayed an undeniable attraction to their part of the property. Whenever I had trouble finding her I would only have to check under the deck at the far end of their house. It seemed like she had adopted that small space down there for her safe zone, and every so often she would even sneak into the house for a wander and a sniff.

As I watched her get more and more edgy about the unusually crowded situation in my place I could only think of one solution: I texted Nickie to ask if they'd be willing to take her until the evacuation was over. Being a very helpful neighbor she replied instantly saying she'd send over Billie to pick her up.

So I opened my patio door with Jazzy in my arms and transferred her over to Billie who was waiting already. There ya go, all done in less than two minutes.

I don't know if any of us realized it that day, but that was Jazzy moving in! Once that dawned on me I was amazed at how this finicky girl was so uncomplicated when it came to changing homes. Yeah, she must have thought, I love you, lady, but your house is *bo-ring!*

I don't take these things personally. In fact, any of my cats, down to my very dearest favorites (even though I have no favorites, haha . . .) would get my full support if they ever showed signs of wanting to live somewhere else. I love them with every fiber of my heart but my pledge and promise from the beginning has always been that I will accept our parting for whatever reason it may come and will simply remain in the space of gratitude and appreciation for having been blessed with their presence in my life at all.

That Jasmine would prefer a house with an active, full family, where there was so much more going on and so many more hands to pet and make a fuss over her seemed only logical knowing where she was coming from. All I needed to verify was that her new family were happy with the arrangement as well so I kept checking with them to make sure.

It didn't take too long before Jazzy got even more company, Mercury, also a gray kitten but with a white patch on his neck. On the odd occasion when I was asked to take care of them I had the opportunity to get to know him better while gratefully deepening my connection with Jasmine.

"Move along. Nothing to see here . . ."

Mercury was quite shy at first but soon came out of his shell, though more towards my food plates than myself. Being so small still, I had to keep him indoors initially, which probably didn't endear me to him an awful lot. He did learn where cuddles were available, but most times he and Jazzy put on first class cabaret shows for me, which were great fun to watch.

So the months passed and eventually Mercury was allowed outside as well. When he'd see me come around the corner or get out of my car he'd make a dash up the deck, because of 'scary monster alert' whereas inside his house he would graciously accept being petted and cuddled. It wasn't me that was the Jekyll and Hyde there, honestly!

Jazzy meantime got herself the best of both worlds, it seemed. In the mornings, if I didn't have to go out anywhere she'd watch for movement behind my patio curtains, and when she spotted me she'd come running. Then I would open the door to let her in so she could do a 'very important inspection'. Once she was satisfied that everything was as it should be she would make it known that she was open to a 'super back scratch spa session', which she'd spend curling her tail and squinting up at me in delight.

"Your house is still too quiet for my taste. Except for that stuff you listen to all the time, that is. One of these days we'll have to have a discussion about that."

Oh . . .? It never occurred to me to ask Jasmine about her favorite online lectures!

"Okay, Jazzy! You're on!"

Now that should be interesting . . .

Bottle Kitties' Trip to the Pub

Having adventures exploring is one of my favorite pastimes and it's even better when you have some fur-baby company. It was no surprise therefore that I jumped on the chance to take a little puppy and two kittens 'over the hill' to San Jose where their weekend foster moms would meet me to collect them.

Yay, a bottle! (Photo: Adrienne Jacques)

The first challenge was to find a good meeting place. I was not that familiar with Silicon Valley and at the time I didn't have a phone with route guidance to help me. Maps and screenshots would have to do the trick.

I thought I had picked wisely and conveniently for the doggie but despite of what I thought were very clear directions the dog foster mom went to the mall opposite of where I was waiting for her. Thankfully a barrage of texts cleared up the miscommunications and we finally succeeded doing the handover.

My next stop was to meet kitty mom at a place and location I had never even heard of before. I found it alright on the second try but to my dismay it was a large grocery store with no shaded parking anywhere. I couldn't even park close to the entrance to wait in order to spot her as soon as she arrived.

I was getting a bit concerned. It was the middle of July, the Valley was baking hot and even though I did have good air conditioning in my car I was worried about overheating, which my old Impala was prone to do. But I really had to find a way to keep the kittens cool.

Now what . . . I took another drive around the area, then walked by the stores for closer inspection but none of the places, not even the coffee shops, had any shaded areas outside where I could bring the kitten carrier.

Finally a picture flashed into my mind and I remembered seeing a British Pub just before I drove into the big parking lot. It might even have a back entrance from a corner of the grounds where I was. When I checked it out, it was right there, all the way in the back.

It turned out that I was further in luck because they even had a patio with parasols. Inside, the pub was dark and smelled of stale beer. Thankfully the bar man allowed me to bring the carrier through to the outside seating. He gave me permission to feed them when I ordered my lunch and a kind waitress brought me hot water for the bottles as I waited for my food.

I took Rosie out of the carrier and was just in the middle of feeding her when I heard a squeak. The waitress had discovered our 'Operation Kitty Bottle'

"OH. MY. GOD! They are so CUTE! Can I hold one?"

"Sure," I said. "If that's not against regulations . . ?"

She looked at me for a second, then shook her head and laughed.

"Too late for that! We've broken just about all of them already . . ." she cooed and awwwed as she picked up Dylan and cradled the tiny baby in her hand.

Both kittens were completely unfazed by the unusual environment. On the contrary, they appeared to feel quite at home. They never complained or cried and just let themselves be petted, admired and spoiled. I was really impressed and felt it was an auspicious sign for a happy weekend break in Silicon Valley. Who knows, they might even pick up a bit of coding while they were there! You gotta start them young these days . . .

So . . . No one could possibly say we're not pulling out all the stops to care for our furry companions. I mean, two weeks old and already they're having bottles at the pub. I was hoping though that it was not an indication of how their lives were going to go.

Dylan: Psst . . . got a beer . . .?

Recently Dylan kitty was in the room when I was doing a reiki session for his mom. As soon as I started he got all excited, purring really loudly. Then he came up close and started to sniff all around me, hands, shoulders and all.

Which now of course makes me think – does healing energy have a scent? Apparently it does!

SADIE AND ELY

Sadie and I had always had a connection though it was more of a distant thing since we didn't see each other that much. Then one day I got a call from her mom letting me know that Sadie had had an accident and was at home with a broken leg. I was asked to come sit with her, help with the care and do some energy healing work.

Her mom Rhadiante had made a beautiful comfy bed in the living room. Sadie was resting on it when I arrived, a big suture running across her back leg. She must have been hurting but took it in her stride, that's how brave a girl she was. After getting caught up on the situation and Sadie's immediate needs I did some pendulum work with her. It was based on emotional release work to help her let go of any shock and trauma she still had in her system, followed by some color light healing. Afterwards I sat and gave her reiki for general soothing and healing support.

Sadie was a lovely patient. She was graceful and appreciative of everything people did for her, it was obvious just by looking into her eyes. Her mom was working with a first class vet, and a number of tools and modalities to help Sadie get through her injuries. She also gave Kangen water for drinking and on the stitches, all of which helped her make great strides in recovery. In the following weeks, I got to spend a lot of time with Sadie. I took care of her food, water and other needs, sometimes we did sessions, and sometimes we'd just sit together. She was always loving and showed how grateful she was for those quiet times of simple presence in the beautiful forest that surrounded the house.

As time went on my visits were required less frequently but the bonus point was that eventually we could go on walks together.

One night I was there to pet sit her, Ely the cat, the ducks and the fish when Sadie came up to me. She had an expectant look in her eyes that I couldn't quite place.

"What is it, Sadie? Do you need anything?" I checked her food bowl and her water but everything was as it should be.

She turned and walked out the doggie door. I followed, curious, to find out what she was after.

It was dark out but Sadie kept going on down the drive. I got my flashlight so I could see where she was going, still wondering what that was all about.

She had slowed down and I was straining to see what she had found.

It was . . . nothing! She was just sniffing!

I laughed and kept following her. That's when it dawned on me. Sadie, the dog was taking me for a walk!

Seriously, Sadie? Has Silver the Cat put you up to this?

I pointed my light in her direction again. Oh my, was I following a coyote there?

No, thank god, still Sadie, who was enjoying this tremendously. She kept walking further down, doing her doggie things along the way.

After a while I saw some eyes glistening in the beam of my flashlight. I hoped that it was Ely the hunter kitty, whose eyes were reflected there, I thought.

"Come on, Ely, let's all go back in the house!" I called.

"Nah, thanks. I'm good. I'll be home in a bit. Got some more stuff to attend to here . . ."

"Aw, come on, we need to turn around, it's late." I called Sadie over my shoulder.

"Time to go home now . . ."

Apparently that was the trick to get her to come because ten seconds later she barreled past me at breakneck speed.

Back at the house she looked at me, grinning from ear to ear.

"Did you have fun?" I asked.

"Ye-e-e-s," she grinned, even wider than before, if that was possible.

I went in and sat on the sofa. Sadie came to join me, and as we settled down cuddling together, I must have fallen asleep.

An hour or so later I woke up. I was very disoriented and had no idea where I was. Looking up all I could see was a bright light and in it a squinty eye Siamese staring down on me from above.

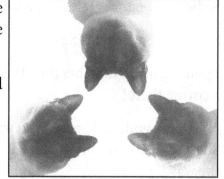

"Finally," I sighed. "I've died and gone to kitty heaven . . ."

Oh Ely, what a clown you can be . . . !

Is this kitty heaven?

Tommy Takes His Place Among Rainbow Kitties

I guess it's pretty obvious that in my mind, all cats are special, but Tommy was definitely something else. For starters, I always had a vague suspicion at the back of my mind that he could actually fly.

Tommy cuddling time!
Ready when you are

Perhaps he was just too clever at fooling me. With his round heavy set shape and adorable bow legs he often looked like he was utterly un- able to move. I'm not really ashamed to say that more often than not I fell for his big soft eyes that pleaded with me to pick him up and carry him to his next destination. But then sometimes I would turn my back for just a bit and in a second or so he had made the jump up to his dinner table or even down to the floor and up onto the kitchen counter, always without the slightest sound. I think I can be forgiven for thinking he might have been able to fly!

His life had been pretty eventful. Having been left behind by his people and facing the prospect of ending up in a shop window in hope of adoption Tommy was spared that fate in the nick of time by his kind, caring neighbors Kathy and Ian who had already adopted some of his siblings and found homes for the others.

Things were not cushy for him or his new mom and dad but apparently he did everything with impeccable style. I am told that when he had to undergo cancer treatment on a daily basis for a month he became the poster kitty at the vet's. Dressed in a sailor suit to stop him from scratching, he had the run of their reception area, was said to help the ladies there with admin tasks (mostly deleting, I think . . .) and was the star of many pictorial updates showing off in all his glamor.

Sailor Captain at the Vet
(Photo: Kathy St John)

Mealtimes with Tommy were never boring. In younger days he would be a menace stealing everyone's food, including that of whatever people were around. Later he just confined himself to yowling really loud when he felt it was his turn. He was definitely an operatic cat boy!

Due to a number of health issues he had to have a syringe full of medication squirted in his mouth, which he usually took without too much of a fight but I could swear there was always a little disgusted *'bleh'* just before I set the dish with his main course in front of him.

Tommy was up for cuddles any time of the day or night, spotting quite quickly when my chores were done and I could sit down for a while. Then he and Donald, the fluffy black cutie, would come running to divide my lap and chest up between them.

Recently Tommy was diagnosed with heart failure that led to fluid build-up in his chest. After another few vet trips Kathy and Ian could see that he was going downhill rapidly and would no longer be able to enjoy even the small pleasures he had left in life. The heartbreaking decision was made to call the vet to the house so that he could get a loving send off in his happy home environment among beloved humans and friends.

Tommy left his body peacefully on his dad's lap accompanied by our tears. It goes without saying that he will never be far from our hearts.

Dear Tommy,

We are here today to ease your suffering and help you make your way over the Rainbow Bridge.

I have only known you for a few short years but have come to love you like one of my own kitties. Your gentle nature, along with your energetic and persistent yowls at meal times, have found their way deep into my heart. I adore your big, deep eyes and your gorgeous ears that are so uniquely your own.

I have treasured every moment that we got to share love and cuddles. Please know that I will be forever grateful for you having been part of your life.

I am sending all my love along with you on this your next adventure.

Perhaps one day we will meet again when you show up as a tiny fluffy kitten or a stray that has finally come home. For now, we wish you a happy family reunion on what we humans call 'the other side'.

Bless you, Tommy!

Tommy
(Photo: Kathy St John)

PART TWO

HEALING

ADVENTURES

or

"Who Heals Whom?"

Healing With The Invisible – What Brodie Taught Me About Energy

Quite early on in our time together, Brodie jumped onto the sofa where I was sitting one day. Wriggling and turning he placed himself so that my hands were on specific parts of his body. He had done that before, and I had learned to recognize it as a sign that he was after some healing.

At first I didn't feel anything happening. I just kept my hands where he seemed most comfortable with them – on his tummy and his back. After a while he sighed and I sensed that a flow of energy had started.

I began to wonder what it was I was meant to be doing and whether I was giving him what he needed, trying to feel if I could pick up on anything wrong with him from the energy that was moving between my hands.

As the thought of what might be wrong with him ran through my mind the word 'correction' appeared and the phrase that came with it was 'God's perfection.'

For the next minute or so I focused on those words.

Suddenly Brodie lifted his head and looked back over my right shoulder, eyes wide open. After a minute or so, he turned, looking over my left shoulder for a while, again with eyes as big as saucers, staring like what on earth is *THIS???*

Then, with another deep sigh, he dropped back onto the sofa, but before his head even touched the cover again he started to purr . . .

EMBARRASSMENT BY INTUITION OR HOW JOSE GOT HIS LEGS BACK

Jose: Ready to Walk the Talk
(Photo: Katie Seeger)

Working with intuition can be a wonderful thing. It is great to receive immediate feedback by way of sensing what is happening with your human or animal client. My intuition however, seems to have some kind of a naughty streak that occasionally delights in putting me in embarrassing situations.

A few weeks ago my client was an adorable little male Chihuahua, Jose, who had trouble using his legs. Disregarding a prognosis of him possibly not being able to walk again his mommy had decided to give other kinds of healing a try. One of them was my emotional release 'Unicorn Code style.'

During our Skype call the web camera was trained on Jose as he was lying there in his little bed, pretty much motionless. Starting with the treatment I identified the first two emotions, which I then proceeded to release for him. Much to my surprise my pendulum indicated that this already completed what I call the 'general sweep', the initial house cleaning that deals with what sits right on top of the heap.

The major issue about Jose was that his leg troubles had made it impossible for him to stand up, which was a big worry for his mom Katie, not in the least because he had not been able to pee in two days. It did not surprise me therefore that once we had worked with the standing up issue, a big part of the session was taken up by emotional releases from the kidney and bladder area. After letting go of a handful of other old emotions 'worthless' came up.

That made sense to both of us. Not being able to stand up and therefore not being able to relieve himself unaided could well demoralize any self respecting Chihuahua.

As I ran my pendulum to clear the unwanted energy off his system I suddenly had a weird sensation. It concerned my 'private parts', so I hesitated for a moment before I spoke.

"Um . . . I have a feeling like I need to go to the bathroom, but I kind of know that I don't . . . ?" I said, chuckling a little.

I was grateful that Katie didn't laugh at me one bit.

"Do you think I should take him outside and see if he wants to pee?"

That sounded like a good idea. "Yes, go for it!"

She folded the cover back that was keeping him warm and started to giggle.

"It's soaked here . . . ! He already 'went'," she called back over her shoulder.

Katie and I both noticed the relief of that, though we agreed that Jose would have felt it most! It was a promising development for his condition, and the change showed up instantly. He had been listless and lethargic to begin with, but now we could clearly see him perk up.

Continuing with the session we found that he had been blaming himself, possible for losing his capabilities but perhaps even more so for the other big issue in his life, the loss of his best and beloved buddy, a cat named Mr Cuddles. A lot of grief related emotions came up for release as we moved on to help him over that sad event in his recent life experience. 'Anger,' 'heartache' and 'resentment' were also part of the mix that this poor doggie had been carrying around.

Eventually we identified 'shock' that had lodged in his energy six lifetimes ago. As he was letting go of it he gave a deep sigh, indicating the nice, solid release of a key emotion.

"Time for a good swig of water!" I said.

Katie went to refill her glass in the kitchen, while I kept my attention on the screen. I watched in amazement as Jose turned his head and looked up at me, straight into Katie's laptop camera. It felt like he was looking me right in the eyes, which was very odd indeed. First of all, because my camera wasn't even on, I was only on audio, but secondly because here was a dog who somehow knew that if you want to look someone at the other end of a web link in the eye, you don't look at the screen, you look into the camera, which is usually right above the screen. Most humans don't even understand that, and here was a little doggie that totally 'got it'. I was impressed!

I called out in delight and started to talk to him, telling him what a wonderful dog he was, and that I was so proud about how well he was doing. His eyes moved, it was almost as if he wanted to hug me whenever I spoke. Of course he couldn't, so he did the next best thing and responded with enthusiastic tail wagging.

For the remainder of the session Jose kept moving his legs and head, stretching, looking around, showing us how much better and how relieved he was feeling – in all ways! At one point it even looked like he was trying to stand up.

I was kind of hoping that he would, but had to remind myself to stay open minded, allow him to do the process at his own pace.

So we proceeded gently, releasing another handful of emotions that were specifically geared to let go of any issues about standing up and being able to support himself. Then we moved on to do a quick sweep for his mommy and his lost buddy.

Whenever I work with pets I find it very beneficial to include their people in the treatment. If there has been a loss in the family I usually make a point to also work on the one that has passed as well. In sessions like that, I see more and more how the energies of animals and their people intermingle. Our bonds are much closer than many of us suspect, sometimes it is as if we are passing emotions back and forth like tennis balls.

The patterns that emerge from these releases are often quite beautiful. We share some emotions, deal with a few of our own, go a few lives into the past and then we reconnect, come back to exchange some more as we help each other on our paths.

If I had ever had any doubts about whether life goes on after the event that we call death, doing this work would have taught me otherwise very quickly. Every time I have done emotional release on an animal that has passed over I have felt the connection strongly because their energy is intact. Just as we can drag old energetic baggage from one life through to the next so can our pets.

That was also the case for Mr Cuddles. Leaving a dear, loving family behind can be hard, especially when their presence has been a reality for so many years. I could tell from the emotions that showed up how his process of passing had started and how he moved through the different stages. Once I had cleared terror, grief, loss of control, anger and confusion from his system I felt the relief of calm and peace from him, and we all knew that wherever he would go from there he could start pretty much unburdened, with a clear and clean slate.

When I contacted Katie for an update two days later, she said that Jose had been feeling much better and more cheerful in spirit but had not been able to stand properly yet. Because he also had not had any bowel movement she had made a vet appointment. We had discussed the possibility in our session. I had recommended a vet visit if she felt any need for it at all. There had been so many emotions on his kidney and bladder that I felt he might need veterinary care. Sometimes that is necessary when we don't catch things early enough.

We did a quick follow up treatment to help prepare him for the visit. He released another whole level of emotions that took quite a load off him. Afterwards I called Katie to see how it had gone and was told to my relief that he had pooped in the car on the way there.

"And right now he's peeing again!"

Yay, I thought, laughing out loud. Looks like I have made a new dog friend, one who is going to pee whenever he hears my voice now!

The good news is that together with some other remedies, Jose is using his legs again to stand and walk. Still a bit wobbly, but he is demonstrating the spirit and the determination to make a full recovery.

The most recent communication I had included a video of him enjoying an almost steady walk around the garden, including doing his 'business'!

Way to go, Jose!

Lil'Bit – A Healing Journey

The other day I was asked to assist a boy kitty whose attitude and behavior had deteriorated over the years. The loss of his best friend and eventual introduction of other pets into the household had been too much for him to cope with. He had taken to peeing in the wrong places until the situation got so bad that he had to be kept in a separate room. Most definitely, an energy healing session was in order . . .

It was a remote treatment via instant messaging and so I started the process of releasing his trapped emotions by getting permission to act as his proxy. Once that was given and the connection made I picked up my pendulum to identify the first trapped emotion, which turned out to be a whole batch: humiliation, jealousy, longing, lust, overwhelm, picked up around age 8-9.

They were all released together. Next came another batch, this one specifically pertaining to kidney and bladder: blaming fear, dread, horror, peeved, all picked up from around age 5-6.

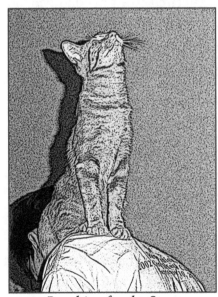

Reaching for the Stars
(Photo: LilBit's Moms)

After that, two single emotions, worry and anxiety, both from age 0-1.

Once those two were released, I noticed something odd: I began to feel bubbly and giggly, almost giddy, and then, all of a sudden, tearful, a need to be held and cradled. That had never happened before.

"Do you have time to cuddle him?" I asked.

"Sure!" said his mom, taking him in her arms.

By now tears were streaming down my face as if they were never going to stop. It felt like a dam had been broken, and a lot of upset was coming out into the open.

Eventually I felt it culminate with a message: "I wasn't peeing, mom . . . I was *crying through my weenie . . .*" and "I am so glad you can hear me now!"

"*I wasn't peeing mom...*"
(Photo: LilBit's Moms)

"He's purring . . . and burbling . . . Seems fine . . . Now he's off grooming himself!"

I felt calmer too, and my tears had subsided.

My pendulum said we still had emotions to release so we continued. The next three batches were all inherited from his daddy, who must have had a really tough time in his own life, too. They were the last ones though.

I was relieved because it had been quite an intense session for the little kitty. Time to digest and integrate!

His mom gave me some information that matched up the timeline with the findings from my pendulum. I was impressed to see how systematic Lil'Bit's treatment had been. He had released the more recent emotions first, going back through the times when a dog and two cats were added to his life before he had been able to deal with the loss of his best friend, all the way back to the first year of his life when his people rescued him from the shelter death row. Only after that was he able to go back to the loss of his dearest Buddy and let go of the anger he had been carrying about that for over five years.

Releasing the anger opened his heart. It allowed him to trust again, and he felt safe enough to communicate to me a sense of wanting to be held. When his mom responded with love and care he could finally connect and release his most major heartache. I had been feeling and crying the tears for him as I received the other messages that almost broke my heart in their simplicity, how it wasn't 'real' peeing but instead 'crying through my weenie . . . '

Cats don't cry the way humans do. The only liquid they have to shed is their urine, which unfortunately is one that upsets their people, especially when we don't understand that it is a communication or when we don't know what to do about it.

At that stage of the treatment, be it for people or for animals, I always feel immensely touched and privileged to be part of such an intimate experience. I can only liken it to the sense of grace and mystery that happens during the metamorphosis of a chrysalis into a butterfly. Releasing our outdated emotions brings us step by step to the experience of who we really are – beings of true love and beauty.

After a transformation of this magnitude I was not surprised to hear that Lil'Bit looked a bit awkward and tentative in his own skin, but he "took to his litter box that evening and stayed as long as he needed to".

I am pretty sure that Lil'Bit will find his own self again pretty quickly. He seems a smart kitty who knows what he wants!

Buddha Zone
(Photo: LilBit's Moms)

Pet Secrets

As always with love, opening your heart to pets means running the risk of sadness, grief and loss further down the line and to me it didn't matter whether I had actually met the furry thing in question or not.

When I heard about a beautiful boy kitty who had been put 'to sleep' due to a growth in his abdomen it made me very sad. I was called for an online emotional release session because apparently one of the female cats in the household had taken the loss quite badly.

Rusty: "I can keep secrets . . . Tons of them!"

In previous treatments this adorable kitty had released a fair number of old burdens that had been troubling her. Now it quickly became obvious, though it still surprised me, how much grief and sadness she was carrying from this recent experience, not just for herself, but for the whole family, including the deceased kitty.

I love to help people and animals feel better, but it also really saddens me to see how far we still have to go in gaining general acceptance for energy work and acknowledging its power. Sometimes I just want to bang my head – *and everyone else's!* – in frustration. Are we really so brainwashed that we can only have faith in preparations that have been cooked up in labs and ignore all the other wonderful and supportive ways we have available to ensure the well-being and longevity of our beloved companions?

There is no way of telling whether that kitty boy would still be alive now if I had got to him sooner. From the results of his treatment I can piece together a little bit of his story which tells me that something bad happened to him at the age of ten months. He had responded with hatred, so strongly, that when I connected to it, it made me want to cry forever. The emotion had remained stuck in his energy system for the rest of his life, almost four whole years. He had already come in with the trapped emotion of self abuse and the combination of the two would have only made it worse. I felt convinced that he was abused when I found that he had also picked up hatred from someone in his environment as a resonant emotion.

At that stage my eyes began to hurt in the back of my head. As a triple whammy hatred came right up again, this time as a past life trapped emotion. My eyes were hurting badly now and the phrase 'blinding hatred' sprang to mind. Once we released that along with some past life worry I felt fine again, a good sign that he had let go of the emotion completely.

When I first started doing this work I was continuously startled by what came up in the sessions, the strength of feelings that needed to be released, even for tiny little kittens and puppies. But I learned very quickly that they experience things every bit as much as we do and my compassion for what they go through, sometimes purely for our sake, knows no bounds these days.

In energy work feelings like hatred and resentment are connected to the liver. When I queried the location I was told that the little black kitty's growth was indeed found in the liver and kidney area. As I said, I have no guarantee that he would be alive now if we had released those energies before the vet pronounced him a hopeless case, but I find myself wondering if his condition might have been treatable, rather than lead to a death sentence.

I feel very sad that I didn't get the chance to at least try and help before it was too late. As it is I could only ease his transition across the rainbow bridge and help his family cope with his loss.

I wonder what it would take for more people to understand that we are not always at the mercy of pharmaceuticals and their limits, that discomfort and disease can often be likened to a traffic jam of blocked energetic issues like old, stuck emotions. These days we have so many tools to let go of blockages, to make energies move freely again and circulate in the way they are supposed to. We can do much to restore balance and well-being in the process, and last but not least, freeing our pets as well as ourselves up again to access our own self-healing.

DEALING WITH THE LOSS OF PETS

Most of us know that losing a beloved pet is just as bad as losing a family member, as a recent study confirmed. Reaching out for help in such a situation is recommended because we often tend to underestimate what is really going on.

About a week ago I was asked to do an emotional release session for a lady after she lost her little dog, who she had been very close to. She wanted help with the grieving process and with feeling better about the turn of events. While we did get to a point of conclusion at the time, we were unable to get her to a place where she felt completely restored to her former self. I suggested that a treatment on the dog might be the missing link.

It may sound strange to think about doing a session on an animal that has passed on but it is helpful to remember that the larger part of us is eternal and that we can carry issues and emotions in our energy system over many lifetimes.

Mary and I got online together late the following night, morning her time. Checking in we cleared a few more emotions for her and then proceeded to work on her little dog Joey.

As I was asking my pendulum about the relevant emotions that could be released at that time my 'rational head' kept trying to interfere. It keeps surprising me how obstinate that internal doubter is, that even after so many years of doing intuitive energy work I sometimes have to assert my true self and tell that voice to stand in the corner and shut up!

We kept releasing a mixed bag of emotions, some evidently connected to how Joey's life had ended – he had to be put down after biting Mary – some going deeper into inherited ones or even way back to tough lives he had lived before.

There was a crucial time in his life with previous owners, around 18 months old, where intense emotions like terror, despair and humiliation needed to be released. When 'failure' came up as 'current' emotion I had tears welling up as I was tapping into the deep sadness of this little doggie who felt devastated about letting his people down.

Whether I have doubt or not during a session, this is usually the time when it disappears in a puff of smoke. These feelings are too strong and too real to be denied, and I am always grateful when they show up because they give me confirmation that we have truly established contact and are on the right track.

The next feeling little Joey communicated to me was immense gratitude for what his mom and dad had done for him in those last couple of years of his life. I was glad to share the message.

"He really appreciates you for being so kind and loving with him."

We were both feeling emotional when this statement came through. Even though my role is to be the messenger in this I always feel touched as I am watching the process unfold.

Next came a sense of not being able to take it any more, not having any strength left to fight his lapse into bad behavior. The poor boy was simply exhausted and worn out.

'Wanting a fresh start . . . ' That emotion made us both want to cry, and right on cue the corresponding one of 'Hopelessness' was released, originating from a past life root event.

After this massive letting go of crucial blocks the next message that came through felt positively heartbreaking:

"It's all right, mom . . . "

"Yes, I know," she said when she could speak again. "But then why is it still so painful?"

"Where is your pain on a scale from one to ten?" I asked.

"Ten," she said, without hesitation.

I checked with my pendulum and found three very deeply hidden emotions from past lives long ago that had to be released before we felt the session was complete.

We then talked a little about the dog she had when we first met, a beautiful greyhound rescue named Honey. I found out that Honey's time with her had also been cut short in a quite dramatic way. I had a sense that the two events were connected, however the session had been intense and both of us were tired so we agreed to address the issue next time.

As I wrote the email with the notes from the treatment I realized I had not checked back about the current pain level, so I added the question, asking Mary if she could tell. She replied she didn't know, that the pain had just 'sort of disappeared'.

Later I found myself wondering why these things hurt so much. A surprising and interesting thought appeared in my mind by way of an answer. My sense was that this was the risk we were taking, that in our love for our animal companions we allow them to break through our shell, perhaps deeper than we do sometimes with our human companions. When our pets leave, especially in such drastic ways as requiring from us to decide over their life and death they crack our hearts open like an egg. They almost force us to give up being safe and rigid asking us to get in the flow, become 'fluid', as we undertake this current, unprecedented shift into our new multi- dimensional reality. It is a labor, or rather, a co-creation of love on both sides. Going through this pain with eyes open holds immense rewards as we expand alongside our hearts.

Witnessing such a connection being revealed in the course of a treatment always feels like a privilege in its beauty and sacredness. Most often the sense of the animal being present in essence and fully engaged is rich and strong. I always come away with a huge feeling of compassion for all that our beloved pets are willing to go through for us, and we for them.

And not once in my experience have they left a session without sending deep love and gratitude for their human family no matter what the events appeared to be on the surface.

My respect for them keeps growing every time I do this.

Mu-Ki: "I have friends in high places!"